PROHVARK

MEHMOOD KHAN MUSA

AURAQ
PUBLICATIONS

Printed in the Islamic Republic of Pakistan.

Printed: January, 2023
Edition: 1st
ISBN: 978-969-749-217-6
Price: Rs 1200 PKR, $12 US

www.auraqpublications.com | raabta@auraqpublications.com
@AuraqPublications | @AuraqBooks | +92-300-0571-530
Printed and Bound by *Passive Printers* - www.passiveprinters.com

PART 1

TEST

It was late in the afternoon when our protagonist awoke. For a few seconds, after opening his eyes, he stared blankly at the ceiling. A thought of getting up and sitting on the chair fleeted through his mind but quickly subsided. He could feel a certain weakness of his body, but he did not turn or twist around to endorse it. And so, a couple of minutes passed by. "Time to get to work, Prohvark!" he said out loud to himself, followed by a sigh. A small, brown circular wooden table, rough on the edges, lay a few feet away from his sleeping corner. He grunted as he exerted a quick surge of energy and quickly sprang to his feet. Walking towards the table, he picked up a glass full of water, not to drink it because he did not feel thirsty but to determine whether it was clean. And to affirm how clean the water was, he brought the cup to his lips and poured in a mouthful. He gargled in his mouth until he appeared satisfied with its condition. Then he curled up his left hand in the form of an arc and spit that same water into the palm of his hand. He began to wash and smear it all over his face, putting special emphasis around the eyes. He suddenly felt a sense of renewed energy within him. His room was about 5 yards from wall to wall at each end, adjoining towards a small toilet that was well-kept and clean at all times, which is why it probably led to clarity of thoughts every time he sat on the toilet wondering. But his room was dusty. And there lay a bunch of miscellaneous objects scrambled around the floor in a disorderly fashion. Things bound to be seen in the room of a person who has lived as a bachelor for a long time. A Couple of CDs, bunch of used tissue papers, a few-days-old plastic bags (which would probably be used again if the need arose), a red blanket with three black parallel lines in its centre, a crumbled chocolate wrapper, couple of wires and objects of similar sorts. Every time Prohvark walked around, there was not a single step he could take without the vulnerability of stepping on something. The objects were in such a mess that even a snake would probably clutter his way across, clumsily halting confused and puzzled in front of them from time to time. But that did not bother or distress him, for he had lived far too long in such a state and had grown accustomed to it. In fact, now it was by choice that he would not clean his room of all the waste. He would often say to himself, "It's my cave and it's to my likings. After all, a clean and tidy room also contributes to the clarity of my mind. But lately, I have been having nothing but a whole lotta leisure time and my thoughts are starting to become a burden for my head. So, the objects that lay on the floor in a clutter can help in the form of obstacles, like walls, that might stop my thoughts from flowing further down the gutter." He lived alone in his room and that gave him the benefit of speaking out loud to himself. It also could have been that living in solitude for far too long, he had formed this shame-inducing habit of talking to himself. Strange enough, at times he would find himself in public, walking down the streets, consumed by his inner thoughts, forgetting that he was not confined to the comfort of his room, and he would utter a few words loudly and then stop in the middle of his sentence, recollecting himself but by then a few watchful eyes would have taken notice of him. He would detect a mocking expression on their faces. And due to this happening on occasions too many, Prohvark upon coming across any face that showed signs of mockery and contempt would immediately get alarmed and question whether he had been talking to himself.

The apartment in which our hero lived as a tenant was located on the first floor of an old three- storied building, the walls of which had visible cracks and grey patches on it. If a person were to stand below on the road and look at the building, he would clearly see the patches, huge enough, from which the paint had peeled off. And besides one of those patches was the window of our protagonist's apartment. And sometimes a random person might see our hero at the window, with a cup of hot coffee and a thoughtful brain, observing the road below where went cars at high speed. In these cars were people of all walks, some going, some leaving. Some alone, and some alone and smoking. Others laughing in a car full with their families and then others who were frowning. And sometimes, Prohvark could also be seen going past the window to take whatever it was that he needed, which was kept upon a table besides the window. And the busy view of the distracting road below would sometimes make him forget what he was looking for.

Just opposite from the building in which his apartment was, separated by the road Prohvark observed, two three-lane diametrical roads with blocks of dull grey brick used as a partition in between them stood a fairly new and well-constructed shiny building about thrice the size of the former, like a giant standing next to a stable of donkeys. On the sixth floor of this nameless building was his office, where for the past four years he worked hard as an employee, from morning till night, along with a group of people who had the same or interrelating forms of job. He had applied for the job and secured it without any difficulties. At the time of his arrival, on the first day, he noticed that the building had just been constructed and most of the flats were vacant. It only took a couple of months until the building was completely filled with tenants and the signs with which a dissection of the old from the new could be established had disappeared. The reason why the brothels are kept clean and well-managed at all times was the reason for a shabby atmosphere of this specific employment building. It was a market for beneficial activities. People coming and going on matters of duty, delivery trucks and pickups, exhausted and sweaty employees on their break hour smoking at the designated areas, the walls suffering from vitiligo due to faded red spit stains of chewed tobacco, and so the building had lost its shine—becoming an ordinary place like any other that failed to arouse a second viewing. Prohvark had established a mechanically punctual routine from office to apartment from the time he had begun working. From morning to late evening, he would sit upon his desk, facing the computer and creating records of merchandise. Their arrivals and departures, the expiry dates on some, goods damaged or lost. Sometimes damaged and then deliberately thrown away while labelling it as lost. Some lost and accounted as collateral damage from which the money was to be extracted. Trivial details of that sort, no longer putting any strain on his mental faculties, led to a sense of fruitlessness. Never had he met any of his colleagues outside of work nor did he find anyone fun enough with whom he could initiate that process. Nor did he dislike them. The conversation mostly remained work-related, short and abrupt. Short because of the depth in content and the abruption for killing the boredom of continuing with such a topic. Only during the half-hour break would the dialog appear to freely flow towards subjects unrelated. Even then the discussion would hold no meaningful value and be forgotten as soon as the hour, which painfully seemed longer, was over. He went through a set of general perspectives in regard to his occupation. At first, Prohvark had a hopeful excitement which eventually led to a hopeless disappointment. He would sense his soul leaving him upon entering the office. But he never found himself complaining. "Maybe because I have no one to complain to," he had said to himself a countless times. But the years grew him numb and accustomed. He became the job. A certain wish of escaping had taken space in his mind, but at the same time, a strong root of fear in the form of a nervous anxiety was also present. He could not conjure up any other plan or mode of occupation. He could not take a decisive step. So, he was just reduced to praying like a criminal on his deathbed asking for a priest in order to achieve consolation and forgiveness for what might occur after he had taken his last breath. So, it had become a matter of death and resurrection for Prohvark himself. While crossing the three-lane roads every day, he would notice vehicles violating the authorised speed limit in a rapid rush of haste, and a craving for rebellious and riotous fantasies would surge in him as well. And in those fantasies, he would turn out victorious, people would cheer for him, call him a champion, tales of him they would tell, and he would smile and laugh out loud before immediately checking himself.

2

Another day of the same. Prohvark sat upon the chair in his cubicle and began his work on the records. A shipment of goods that are unworthy to mention were wrongly weighted and needed rectifying. It took about fifteen minutes of altering and then editing again. Another box of shipments mislabelled and the same and once again. In such a way, half his day was concluded.

Now the lethargic employees began getting up from their chairs, to start their midday ritual of gathering around to smoke and have their cup of caffeine. They would rarely have anything to eat, electing to have refreshments only. At the smoking stand, Prohvark was surrounded by the familiar faces. The three colleagues with whom he shared his office cubicle. Prohvark had told himself once in the beginning, "Well, I'm sharing the office desk with them so I might dust the ashes of cigarettes along with them as well." And so it had become. Thousands of days and cigarettes ten times more compared to them, but the circle remained the same. The corners were occupied with a circle of employees engaged in the same old vain activities, wasting both their times and primes together. Now as Prohvark was standing there, he noticed something which had never occurred to him before. He noticed those circles never had an assembly of more than four people, in alignment, so did the number of desks and chairs confined to the office cubicle, which were also restricted to four employees. And the realization dawned upon him: people were not familiar with each other or talked to anyone outside the chamber of their own cubicles. The extent to which he was connected with his colleagues, the relationship which was devoid of any real compassion, was the same amongst the rest around him. And the thought of this gave him comfort, to think that he was not alone in his feelings of detachment. That the rest felt isolated too. In this stupid selfish way of projecting his inner depravity on others, making them a vessel that shared his emotions as well, he found comfort and a shifty devious smile spread across his cheeks.

"Uh oh, I forgot the pack. On my desk," said Mike wryly. He was already shifting his body towards the building entrance as he muttered, "be right back!" with his back turned towards the group.

"I hate to waste five minutes out of my hourly break due to your forgetfulness," said Rodric in a dispatchful way.

"But you are surely going to waste away the rest of your break and potentially a couple of years of life by smoking them," thought Prohvark to himself as he brushed aside a patch of dust from his tie.

Ross, the third colleague, with a bloated stomach and an amiable face, had the most petty and insignificant existence in the eyes of Prohvark and the eyes of others from the perspective of Prohvark. His presence was usually forgotten as soon as he was physically out of sight, similar to that of the ash that fell from the cigarette. He had never expressed his opinion in any matters, whether matters of low or high implications, work-related or not, his liking towards any brand of cigarettes, or the colour of a tie. Prohvark had previously sometimes marvelled at this and wondered whether Ross even knew of such thing as an opinion or even a personality. And once again, Prohvark reflected upon those thoughts as he laid his eyes upon Ross who was leaning with the grey dusty sole of his left foot against the wall, his tie tightened around the neck till the point of discomfort, gazing at Mike as he made his exit in towards the building.

"Has our office been shifted to the ninth floor?" said Rodric sarcastically, as he sensed it was taking Mike longer than it should have. Ross who failed to apprehend the remark at first, quickly started surveying the windows of the building and the office with a puzzling expression in order to affirm whether there were any actual movements or clearing of the office equipment. "That's close to ten minutes of my break wasted. NOT five, not FIVE!" splashed Rodric. He was steadily growing impatient with every passing minute until Ross tittered with his characteristic mannerism of bodily assurance upon the sight of Mike who reappeared, exiting the building entrance with quick steps, a cigarette already lighted, held tightly at the right corner of his lips, blowing smoke out through the nostrils. Rodric let out a sigh of dissatisfaction and expressed that a great injustice was done to him for he had waited and was not allowed to be the first one who would light up the cigarette. His expression accused Mike of selfishness.

"I'm late," Mike said as he was closing in from the distance and he sensed their disapproval. "But get this, as I was going through my desk, suddenly it occurred to me that I had left the pack of cigs in the washroom. So, I made my way towards the washroom. And once I made it down there, upon entering, I was caught by a pleasant surprise. Instead of the usual stench of shit, I was able to smell the sweet smell of cigarettes all over the place. Now you may say there is no difference between the repulsive smell of crap compared to that of cigarettes. But let me assure you of the difference, that is I can distinguish between the sweet smell of my brand choice compared to the smell of others. But when it comes to shit, they all smell the bloody same. Except to be specific, if it's bloody..."

At this point, Rodric who was sprouting impatiently for a spark, interrupted Mike by snatching the packet rather abruptly from his hand. Before lighting up, he said, "Will you get to the point now?" which came off as a command.

"Alright. I was damn sure of the smell. They were mine. I could see smoke emitting from one of the toilets, so I held my ground and majestically thought to myself, 'let him enjoy this one'. For I knew the fun of taking a shit while smoking one. Finally, the door opened. And there was our smoker. I caught him red-handed. Or stinky handed. The cleaner. Hah." Mike let the smoke out and resumed, "To tell the whole damn truth, I was relieved at first to find the cigarettes, and just in time too, you see, certainly if it was someone else, they would have made off with it. High chances even the cleaner was gonna pocket them for himself. So, get this, I gave the cleaner a proper lecture and a scolding. You can never pass on over opportunities like this. I said, 'YOU are here to CLEAN the toilet, not POLLUTE IT!' And then I drowned him in threats of complaining to the authorities. I made him think of the probable situation of finding himself in the state of unemployment. The poor guy's face was stretching through all four corners as he began his pleading and appeals for forgiveness. I almost was in fear that he would wet his pants, but luck was on my side or rather his, for we were in the toilet and occasion such as that was not bound to arise. I would have excused him in that case to relieve himself and resume the lecture when he returned. Anyway, sensing an upper hand, I decided to use it towards my advantage. I ordered him to pay me cash, the amount equivalent to that of two whole cigarette packets, OR ELSE! His face found their way back to the centre, upon me offering him his way out of the situation."

"So you extracted money from that dirty poor man? A dictator move," said Prohvark with indifference.

"Yes, I did. Like I said, you must never risk passing over opportunities like those. Specially in a job like ours, where you never get a bonus or an extra to the base salary. But I wasn't completely selfish. I gave the cleaner a couple of tips as well before exiting. Tips on how to quit and overcome the addiction of cigarettes. From the looks of him, he didn't appreciate me giving those pointers. Aah, never mind that. At least, I have surely taught him a lesson on why not to ever smoke in a toilet. And lessons don't come for free nowadays," Mike concluded this with a smile thick with ethical self-satisfaction. He felt completely assured of having not committed an act or any act of a wrong nature.

"Is there a point to all this?" said Rodric without even having searched for the point or even being interested in one.

Ross who had listened with great attention so far walked away suddenly towards the office with an air that implied he had mistakenly associated with a group he did not know. No one cared enough to stop or ask him where he was going. There was still time remaining of the hourly break. Time enough to smoke a dozen more.

"Yes, there is a great point," said Mike. "I have been promoted on an account of all this debacle. Would you believe this into getting it! As I was making my way downstairs, a voice called out to me from the back. It was Boss. Seems like he was inside one of those occupied toilets. And he acted as a secret spectator while I was thundering my lecture upon the good old cleaner. Boss seemed very satisfied with my actions. He voiced his satisfaction. He said I acted like a businessman. A good businessman. Boss also went as far as saying that I acted like an eco-friendly businessman. True that I say most of all. And congratulated me upon the promotion. My time with you guys is short. Sad!"

A promotion, Prohvark thought to himself, *Been a long time since anyone got one. Been the only time I understand why and how someone got one. Maybe the 'no smoking' signs are displayed in toilets to stop the chances of people getting promoted. Maybe people who got fired, got fired because they failed to give an advice to someone suffering from addiction.*

"Did you say something?"

"I said congratulations. You might be the only one who deserves this," said Prohvark joyfully.

A look towards the circle of employees showed signs of them, beginning to slowly disperse one by one, making their way, finding their way, towards the nameless building. Mike squashed his cigarette against the wall, Rodric kicked his towards the trash can and they all made their way towards the office as well.

3

Later in the day, there were talks of a promotion party, at the top of which was Mike making all the decisions in regards to the preparations. He straight away decided that the party was to be held in his own apartment, without even bothering bringing in other locations into the discussion. To justify himself, he proclaimed snobbishly that there was not a hotel upon earth which could match the heavenly comfort and cosiness of one's own apartment. Rodric asked, "Whose apartment that might be?" Upon which Mike replied that he was of course talking of his very own and their apartment was nothing in comparison to his. It was both an insult aimed at their current living conditions and their state of heavenliness in the afterlife. And among the people invited were Rodric, Prohvark and Ross. An invitation was also sent to the Boss and his assistant. But everyone knew they did not care enough to even respond, let alone attend the gathering. Prohvark thought Mike had carefully planned the invitation, knowing well they were likely not to be responded with any sentiments, just to appear grand and ambitious in the eyes of his colleagues.

A moment was also taken in order to discuss whether invitations to people from other departments would be led forward or not. Mike quickly despised the idea, giving a few reasons of an awkward nature, when the underlining motive was to reduce as much expense as he could. And the reasons or rather the excuses invented by Mike were to an extent absurd in such a way that made the underlying reasons of stinginess clearer in the minds of everyone except Ross. For nothing can be determined about him unless and until he nods. It was decided that a cake was also to be presented. Mike wished to have the flavour and toppings of his own liking. And since no one knew what Mike fancied, they were appeased when he put himself in charge of this task as well. Eventually, it was Mike alone coming up with all the schemes and the others just went along with it without sharing any forsaken opinions. They were stopped at the first word which they uttered. Prohvark had already conjured up a mental image of what the party would feel like. Empty, boring and over before he knew it. The last part gave him a fraction of relief and comfort which translated to a smile upon his face.

"What do you say we invite the good old cleaner as well?" Mike said excitingly, "After all, I could not even imagine a scenario of promotion, if not for the old chap caving in to my sweet pack of smokes. Perhaps people will consider whether smoking really is bad for them when they hear of the basis due to which I got my promotion. Yes, I must invite him," Mike decided with no attempt to listen to the feedback.

Is this your way of compensating the poor fellow after you insulted him and robbed him off a couple dollars? Thought Prohvark, deep within the layers of his mind. *The guy deserved and deserves neither. Neither the insult nor the invitation. Perhaps the invitation might serve him another wound, looking into the fact how you achieved the promotion by stepping over him. Or perhaps it might serve as a compensation.*

"Have you considered giving him back what you took from him?" inserted Rodric.

"I have taken nothing," burst out Mike, "I have given punishment and that too rather of a soft nature, in accordance with the blunder committed. And I was kind enough to give a valuable advice on breaking the chains of addiction as well"...Ross shifted his body with approval to Mike. Later, Mike did think of returning what he had taken from the cleaner in all honesty. But he could not come upon a definite conclusion and let the matter subside.

And so, the essentials of the gathering were determined. A bottle of champagne. Two bottles of whiskey. Dinner that was to be ordered. And various other elements of a party that make it the party. Mike also found it necessary to voice some rules for behavior, basic etiquettes, as the party was to be held in his very own apartment. And the rules further convinced Prohvark that the party was to be dull. Mike went out and inquired after the cleaner, found him and invited him personally. Upon returning, he informed the group that the latter was delighted for he rarely received any kinds of invitation at all and the last time he ever attended a party, that he could not remember. The time was set. A day later, tomorrow, straight after work. And a day after that, Mike was to be promoted, leaving an empty seat at the cubicle. Now Mike was to have a room, a small office of his own, with a desk and a leather chair that span around. Precisely why the spinning feature was given to the chair was because the person sitting upon it did not have much productive work on his hands and therefore needed something to kill the boredom with, so he would spin around and fan himself. It was well known that individuals who got the promotion would no longer associate with their old group. Mike was to come later than the rest, enclose himself in the room, and leave earlier before the time everyone else had left. Or sometimes, he would leave whenever he felt like it. So, they did not see each other much. The times he would see them or anyone was on official matters, whereupon they had to ask for and require approval, knocking on his door or through the phone. Mike would open the door, take the papers, sign them or conduct whatever decisions he had in his capacity of undertaking. Sometimes, he would refuse appointments and delay them with no adverse effects. The party almost served more as a farewell party rather than that of a promotion. But farewell to what and from what actually? The old position was no different than the new. Just a facade which seemed better because it paid better. Before promotion, Mike was forced to have a seat in a cubicle of four people. Just a seat. There was no other needs of sharing and compulsion that comes from within. He was solo amongst four people, now he was solo in his room. Friendless as it were. As he were. And he was. With no intention of changing. And no goals of improving.

The preparation to shift Mike and his table equipment had now already begun. And by tomorrow, they would be over. There would be no sign left as to whether the position was occupied before or had it been vacant all along. And then a newcomer would soon occupy the seat, bringing his equipment that were the exact same compared to that of Mike's.

Why even shift those equipment? Get yourself a batch of new ones and hand over the used old ones to the person soon to take over your empty place. So you nullify yourselves from the trouble of shifting. Thought Prohvark, as he was looking at the two helpers busy in a work which could have been avoided. But there is so much unemployment that the unemployed demand to work and make work out of nothing, just in order to have something that they can do. One person can do the job of ten, but he must confine himself deliberately to do the job of five, just so others can also be chained up to a form of activity.

"That's a splendid idea, Prohvark. It should have occurred to me before. But it's hardly too late now. Keep those ideas floating in the air and you might wear the shoes of promotion as well," said Mike jestingly as he slapped Prohvark on the back of his shoulder. Perhaps, Mike genuinely thought that Prohvark was in a race of competition with him.

Prohvark was lost at first. He looked at Mike with an expression of shock and bewilderment, lips slightly parted. He figured he had thought to himself. He was sure he had thought to himself, but not anymore as he watched Mike walking away. The equipment left in their place. Prohvark was consumed by the sound generating from the clicks of keyboards as Ross was typing away seemingly like a mad raging pianist. For a while, he stared at Ross's long and thin fingers as they made their way swiftly across every corner of the keyboard and back again. Then he sensed Rodric was looking at him in a scrutinizing manner. And slightly, with a sense of hesitation, Prohvark resumed to continue upon his working desk as well.

4

On his course towards home, Prohvark was deep thinking. Deep thinking for him was a state in which he would completely become unaware of his surroundings, and it would have to take something loud or sudden to make him come back to the present reality. But he would feel an instant dislike and enmity towards anything that disturbed him from his lack of regard to the external environment. And the fact he would regard the object that bought him back to reality with contempt was a proof enough that he cherished his inner world of being. If the reason was a growling cat, he would curse and spit upon it. And a furious attempt to kick would probably follow later. And if it was wailing toddler, he would quickly offer him a lollipop so he could shut up. Or he would just walk away to a place where the screaming voice of the toddler could not reach. Prohvark was deep thinking about the party now. What were the consequences of him attending and the opposite—sleeping out on it. Excuses he had to make. And now he was thinking about getting promoted himself but leaving out of grandeur every preparation in regard to his promotion party in the hands of his colleagues. Of what might the cake possess a flavor like and how would the aftertaste be. In this state, he made his way towards the apartment. Entering it, he took a seat next to the wooden table. He spent a few minutes staring blankly at the wall and then took to surveying the room, upon which he felt a certain kind of detachment towards this place, this place in which he had spent a little less than five years of his life. Prohvark could not remember what he ate the last time. He was not hungry. Slowly, he picked up the jar of water and halfway filled the cup next to it, he sat staring still again. Floating thoughts occurred aimlessly.

I must soon transition away, progress from those sentiments. Detach myself from them, so space for transmutation can be established. The cup that was dirty, I have filled carelessly with water. And when I was thirsty, I left myself no decision but to drink from it. I'm sick. The water was contaminated with infection due to the messy cup. Now the cup must be emptied from its contents, exactly at that point will I be able to fill the vacancy in me.

Prohvark lifted the glass up and hurled it towards the wall. The shattering noise of the cup splitting into a thousand pieces pierced his ears, and he was back in the present moment. Then he greedily gulped down the water straight from the jar, with a stream of it squeezing its way from around the corner of his lips and dripping down to his lap. He got up and threw himself on the bed and quickly fell asleep. Later, just in time, he awoke to have another day at the office. As he was exiting his apartment, he glanced around quickly and to his surprise there were no pieces of shattered glass or accumulated water. He was unsure whether he had been dreaming or not, but he dismissed the whole thought, for he was very pleased at not having to clean the floor. Or to walk with the fear of stepping on broken glass and hurting his feet, even to step upon it with his shoes appeared distasteful because of the unpleasant noise that the crumbling glass would create when once stepped upon.

Another day at the office was soon to be over. There were no talks regarding the party at all and no one seemed excited about it. Mike was not to be seen around the cubicle. He had spent the day in his new office, busying himself, putting things together. During the break, Rodric refused to go out for a smoke and Ross nodded. So Prohvark exited the building alone, with the intentions of taking a stroll. Down below, he saw the same old cleaner near the entrance of the building, sitting on the stairs, his broom tilted next to him along with his can of trash. His yellow uniform was dusty and dirty, he looked tired having cleaned all the corners he had to clean, and his dark brown legs were extended for some rest. The cleaner was not old enough to deserve all the wrinkles on his face. It was only that he had lived a life of hardship. The dust flew throughout the day as he was working and landed on his face only to intermix with his sweat and ended as a mixture that seeped deep inside the wrinkles of his forehead, deep enough that it would take a toothpick to dig them out. Prohvark pitied him as he walked across. Later, in the middle of him taking a stroll, a certain trick occurred to him that he would play on the cleaner. Approaching the entrance of the building at the near end of his break, he caught sight of the cleaner from a distance who was still sitting in his old position. As Prohvark mounted the first set of stairs, he placed both his hands in the pockets of his jeans, and in one of the pockets was the packet of his cigarettes. Then he deliberately let the packet slip and slide away from his pocket, which fell on the basement a couple of paces away from the cleaner. With gleaming eyes, the cleaner caught sight of this. But he did not shout back at

Prohvark for recollection. Instead, he quickly snatched the packet off the floor to keep for himself, and to hide it from Prohvark's sight, he stamped his left foot over it, flattening it out as soon as it fell down. Prohvark saw the act as he looked back from the corner of his eyes. He even heard the packet crumble under the dirty shoe. Later, he could not decide coming up with a good reason as to why he had decided to conduct this experiment. But he did conclude that the cleaner did not learn from the experience that occurred in the washroom. As Prohvark resumed on the working desk, he did not talk about the experiment to any of his colleagues and kept it only to himself.

At the near end of the day, Mike came out of his new office and the group saw him for the first instance that day. He came out pretending with a body language that implied he had worked hard throughout the day, and he began right away to remind them of the party which was forgotten since they talked about it yesterday. They were to attend an hour later from exiting the office. Mike's apartment, in which the party to be held, was located at a walking distance of fifteen minutes from the nameless building. It was also known that Mike was to be offered a new apartment that came along with the promotion. An apartment that was offered for the sake of convenience, at a much nearer distance from the office. Whether he would accept the offer was not known, but it was most likely the case of a refusal in order to eliminate the convenient aspect of it for the workers, as they preferably used the excuse of a longer distance to sometimes arrive late at work.

Everyone cheerfully promised they would arrive on time.

Prohvark wore a new, bright blue tie and thought of polishing his shoes, but later he did not make an attempt. Keeping in mind that he was to walk over to the party and they were likely to get dusty again. So he wore them as they were.

Fifteen minutes later, Prohvark arrived at the building where Mike's apartment was located, on the first storey. It was a nicely constructed building according to modern standards and much better in comparison to his own. Taking his way through the stairs and arriving at the brightly lit corridor, he noticed Ross at the apartment door. Ross was wearing a sky-blue, well-ironed shirt, a shirt old but which he was seen wearing only once with a curious face and that was long back on the first day of his appearance at the office. So long ago, he had worn the shirt that perhaps no one had the memory of him wearing it and hence it appeared new. Ross was in the act of pressing the doorbell but stopped just in time, for the sound of Prohvark's footsteps approaching closer were audible enough for Ross to look back and notice him. Ross with a new shirt waved his hand and smiled the same old smile as a signal of a friendly greeting made between people who are on equal terms, but the gesture was done so awkwardly that it made him appear more as a doorman, a porter who performs minor services for recipients and takes the guest towards where they can sit.

Prohvark smiled back and waved in return, and Ross rang the doorbell. They waited for the door to open so they could enter together.

5

Mike opened the door with a sigh, whether it was a sigh of invitation or disgust was hard to say. "Please come in," he said in a low and lazy voice. Both Prohvark and Ross attempted to enter in haste at the same time, whereupon they awkwardly collided shoulders with each other and got stuck in the doorway. Ross made a quick retreat and let the former enter first, after which he followed along, shutting the door behind him rather blatantly, which raised a few eyebrows.

"Quite a theatrical entrance you have accomplished. You must be excited," pitched in Rodric, who was already in the room having arrived first and prior to the appointed time. Rodric attended with his usual working attire without a single addition made to it. This realization made Prohvark a little uneasy. He had doubts whether he had overdone it with the new tie. Whether he appeared as a show-off. And in his uneasiness, he wiped his forehead with the new tie even though he was not sweating in the least bit. He would have gently put the tie back down and patted it into position. But he feared it would seem like he was boasting and trying hard for them to notice his new tie. So, he clumsily dropped down the tie, and it swayed a bit to the left and then to the right and once again. Now he touched it again to stop the movement. He felt himself going red.

"I thought I would wear a new tie for the occasion," inserted

Prohvark to appease his tension.

"Thanks, I guess."

HAH, what a splendid homage you have provided. Are they not glad now that it's not you who is being credited with a promotion, for then you would have dressed yourself up with the adornments and jewels of a clown. Quieten. Said Prohvark to himself.

Rodric had positioned himself comfortably on the only sofa in the room. Laid back, legs laid out the length of almost the entire sofa and crossed. It did not even cross his mind that perhaps he was occupying way too much space on the only relaxing spot in the room. Ross who was gawkily looking around for a place to sit on walked across one corner and then back again. There were two additional chairs around a table, but on the top of one was kept the shiny bottle of champagne and on the other were two bottles of cheap-looking whiskey. All Ross had to do was pick them up and lay them across the table, but in his gawkiness, the idea did not occur to him. So having decided that there was no suitable place for his bum to rest upon, he approached the sofa and chafed himself uncomfortably between Rodric's feet and whatever little space there remained of the sofa. He narrowly missed sitting on Rodric's big and stiff toe. The nail of which was long enough for it to snap in half. The nail would snap in half, not Ross. The party for Ross would have been over there and then if that was the case. Later, Ross saw Prohvark placing the champagne on top of the clothed table and taking a seat comfortably on the chair that was left vacant. He probably thought he could have done that as well. Or plausibly, he could still do that with the other chair. But nothing can be said of Ross and his thoughts, unless and until he nods.

The lights were set at a shade lighter. Lighter than what it was usually set in. It was supposed to give vibes of leisure and relaxation. But that did not help our protagonist at all. On the contrary, he felt tensed and agitated. *Complete darkness and candles might have done the trick. A romantic promotion night.* He sarcastically thought to himself. But knowing Mike, he would have refrained in his stinginess to establish such an atmosphere even on his first honeymoon night. Instead, he would boast and give a lecture to his partner and hope to acquire a promotion, a dominant position in their relationship.

The cake placed in the middle of another table, a table low enough, barely reaching the height of a human knee, was made of chocolate with rainbow-colored sprinkles on top and dark brown cookies made but of much refined and higher quality chocolate compared to that of the cake. Small pieces of cut-up chestnuts could be seen inside and out, in no particular order. Everything was chocolate. No signs of any other flavor. Whether it was so because much importance and thought was not given at the selection or whether it was because Mike only liked and preferred chocolate cakes does not matter. Maybe it was because Mike wanted to appear humble and courteous on his promotion party, so he chose a cake that was simple enough to project that image.

"Are we going to cut the cake first? Or pour the bottle of wine?" asked Rodric since it was a while without any activity having taken place.

"First of all, it's a champagne, not wine, and it's of the highest quality. A champagne made in France. And not just from any place in France. It's from Paris, France. And not brewed just from any place in Paris, France. I have heard it was brewed right under the famous, the splendid Eiffel Tower," Mike said this as he picked up the bottle from the table with both his hands, fondling it as it were his own child. Bringing the bottle closely to his face, it seemed as though he was going to plant a kiss upon it but then thought the better of it. Then he carefully placed it back upon the table, making sure it was not close to the edge, eliminating the dangers of it falling to the ground. Then he turned around facing Rodric while pointing at the bottle, "They say drinking a cup or two, more than enough, could possibly and magically teleport you over the Eiffel." He swung his hand around and now pointed at Rodric's nose with determination, "So be very careful there, buddy"

"Second?"

"Yes, I do firmly second that."

"No, I meant...you were gonna say something else besides selling the champagne like you are being paid the amount of an expert advertiser."

"Uhh...yeah. The second thing, we are neither gonna cut the cake or drink as of now. We must wait, kindly enough, for the boss and his assistant to arrive before we begin the ceremony," Mike said this and walked towards the window. Brushing aside the curtain with two fingers, he looked out pretending they would arrive soon.

"Oh, Come on. You very well know as well as we do. The

superiors don't associate with us low-level employees. There has never been a case. Them arriving at this party is like an eagle which came home to a pigeon's nest, filled with pigeon eggs," said Prohvark. Ross nodded.

"We must wait anyway. So we don't have to lie later that we did not. I have taken the effort of initiating the invitation anyway. Patience. Also speak for yourself, I'm no longer as low as you are," the last remark Mike voiced quickly and thoughtfully as if he had already rehearsed it. "I suppose I am currently the wings of the eagle you talk about. Or perhaps one of the feathers." He added grandly in an attempt to sound philosophical.

"Now you care about honesty. An honest man. A requirement for the promoted huh?"

"A requirement for anybody and everybody out there. Regardless of their occupation. If you were honest enough yourself, you would realize that you have no competency that commends a promotion. I'm much more talented in maintaining my honesty than the rest of you," cried Mike.

"As if honesty was something that required maintaining with talent. And to think you haven't even had a glass to drink yet but have floated towards grand, lofty and heavenly dimensions of virtues, let alone the Eiffel Tower. A man such as you should not be allowed to set rules for behaviors. Not even rules for behavior in your own territory, for it might serve in a cause more damaging towards your own well-being, as is clearly the case. You have set the rules by your speech...And," Here Prohvark was interrupted. And good for the reader because he was becoming to sound like an employed from nine am to six pm version of Friedrich Nietzsche. And imagine how depressingly dull and deep that would have been.

"That's enough, gentlemen. Look, there is a knock on the door".

The door was in fact knocked. More than the crisp knocking sounds, Ross nodding and pointing in assent was proof. It wasn't just any ploy by Rodric to put a halt to the argument which he certainly found amusing. But who would knock on a door, with an attached doorbell. Was this a metaphor by a highly intelligent person or was it just an act of an uneducated mind.

After a moment passed in silence, Mike approached the door and opened it to find the cleaner in his yellow uniform who had arrived late. From Mike's expression, it seemed as though he had completely forgotten inviting him. But here he was, and he was let in along with the broom and bucket which he had bought with him. Mike had a bad taste in his mouth. For him it, felt like he had eaten leftover chicken along with the bones. Having trouble greeting or providing compliments to the promoted, the cleaner with an awkward smile walked and deposited himself in a position close to the corner. It must also be added, the only reason he showed up to the party was because of the stigma and the fear that comes with the refusal of an invitation made by people who are admired or hold a position superior to one's own.

"Alright, gentlemen," said Mike generously, "As we have waited long enough for the superiors to arrive and they have not, I suppose they are going to miss out on the grand party that is about to take place. Some people just don't know how to have fun. We will cut the cake first."

So the superiors did not arrive. And Mike had a bitter feeling that if perhaps he had begun cutting the cake sooner, he would have eaten more. But now the cleaner, that old chicken had come to peck on the crumbs as well. Now they gathered around the cake and Mike sliced through it, cutting a piece out of it which he immediately deposited in his mouth and began chewing. He carved another piece slightly larger than the first one and quickly ate that as well. Wiping his mouth with the back of his hand, he left the cutting knife next to the cake and retreated towards the window where he lit a cigarette and opened the window for the smoke to be blown out. And he spoke back to them with a wave of his hand to carry on with the rest. He commanded in such a manner which implied that the cake had lost all its value and taste since he was done with it. Rodric picked the knife up and cut himself a piece, then he handed over the knife to Ross and he did the same. Prohvark gestured at the cleaner, calling him and bidding him to have his share as well. A small part of the cake remaining at the table needed no cutting. The cleaner stuffed it in his mouth. Showing dissatisfaction at having got a smaller share, he also greedily scavenged the crumbles and every sign that remained of the cake. If only he would clean dirt as swiftly as he had done with the cake, the nameless building would also appear as clean as the slate upon which the cake was kept. Rodric pointed at the bottle of champagne with a greedy smile on his face. Mike picked it up carefully and slowly with both his hands. He gave it a good shake and tried uncorking the bottle which was stuffed in rather tightly. The first few attempts at uncorking, he had failed, and in his frustration, he gave the bottle a good vigorous quaking again. Then impatiently, he twice hit the top of the bottle where the cork was against the table in an attempt to loosen it up. When he tried again, the cork flew out, opening with such a force that it hit the roof of the room and fell upon the cleaner's head and finally jolted towards his feet. The cleaner quickly picked and pocketed the cork up instead of throwing it in his waste bucket. It seemed to him that it was of value. The champagne started gushing out with a high velocity, as if it was drunk upon himself and was aiming for the famous tower and Mike watched the foam with amazement. In his excitement, he forgot the luxury and importance of the highly esteemed champagne of which he himself boasted and was letting it foam and drip down to the floor, letting it go to waste. He held the bottle now in one hand and swiftly moved it around Ross's face, so closely that Ross smelled it and it almost hit the tip of his nose and Ross fell back timidly in a nervous, disturbing retreat. Now the former further swung around in circles with the foaming bottle in his hand, laughing fiercely as he did so. The cleaner who was in awe of the shiny and luxurious looking bottle, with green and golden labels, never having seen any other champagne as close to the colossal quality of this one, nervously fidgeted around watching the bottle closely with wide, strained eyes in fear that it might slip and shatter. Once or twice, he almost made an attempt to stop Mike from the childishness he displayed. Even Rodric was on the edge of his seat. Apparently, he was eager and aroused enough to taste the champagne himself after Mike had gloated about it. Looking now at the bottle being waved and wobbled around gave him pangs of anxiety. Mike stopped at length after rotating close to a dozen times in circles. The champagne had stopped foaming. But he only began.

Looking up at the roof, Mike brought the bottle straight to his lips and started gulping the champagne down. He held the champagne and gulped for a good five seconds, after which he announced, "This is for the sake of toasting. I shall fill the cups for all of you. And you must toast for the sake of me. You flunkies." For some reason, he began to show signs of anger at his colleagues. Perhaps, there was a text on the champagne which said that it was appropriate only for the promoted to consume. And since Mike claimed to be a very honest man, he might have felt that he was betraying himself by offering it to them. Perhaps there was no label, and he was angry due to his innate nature of being a stingy man. "You flunkies." he muttered again but to himself from under his breath. Mike was approaching the table now upon which there were empty glasses kept for the sake of filling. He took a couple of steps but with an effort to take them correctly. He had swung around fast. And now he felt giddy, and a sense of lightheadedness overtook him. The walls were spinning around. Mike tried fixing his eyes upon the cleaner and saw the cleaner with the broom held in his hands, supposedly in an attempt to wipe some stain off the floor. And Mike burst into a stream of laughter upon the sight. He spoke and some of the words he uttered came out awkwardly, as he had begun to grow tipsy.

"Some guys just can't get over the work mentality. Even at holidays and parties. I knew a guy who worked at the travel agency, and during vacations, he used to go traveling himself. Such a queer fellow he was. And there was another one, a clown who worked at the circus. His act was to walk upon a tightrope, balancing himself for the pleasure of the audience. They would throw coins at him, and he would succeed every time. He amassed a good fortune throughout those years of tightrope walking. But one day, he was at home on holiday. After waking up from sleep, a good night's, he slipped while trying to descend two puny stairs making way to his kichhan. Upon slipping, he burst his head open on the concrete. He was found hours later, head buried in a pool of blaad. And thinking that death was approaching him, he kept repeating his last wish, which was that people must never find out that he take the slip while ascending steps. For he thought it was shameful, a tightrope walker, and one such he was, who never slipped whaal walking on a rope, would meet his end in such a easy way. A crowd gathered and carried him to the hospital, and he spent two months in a state of coma. After all that time when he finally arose to consciousness, he also harose to bad news. He was sadly informed by the doctors that he could not again resume his former occupation of tightrope walking. The tightrope walker jumped habashed from his bed, asking to assess the judgement once more with grave pleadings and wailings. "This must be mistake," says he. "I can't live without the rope, and without it, I'm as good as hanged till death. Tell me to nevah come no where near across any stairs instead and my whole life I will avoid them like a plague, even though stairs can be found all ova the place, it's much of a tough feat to avoid them, as for ropes one has to make a deliberate effort to tie them from two different ends. Plhease! So he cried. Look here! Drop that broom, NOW!" Mike pointed with a sudden shift of drunken anger in his tone, "Or I shall have you thrown out. OUUuut! Output. I put you out. I don't want any funny incidents happening at my party and in my apartment." But the cleaner was nowhere near his broom and the rest of them present thought correctly the combination of swirling around in addition to the gulping down of the special champagne had already got to Mike's head. Resuming his walk towards the cups again, he missed a couple of steps and was on the verge of having slipped but quickly recollected himself with a proud gesture and raised his hand in assurance. "Careful now, Careful." Said Rodric. And the next moment, Mike's feet were in the air, slumping down with a thud to the ground, loud enough for the sound to appear pleasing to the ear of anyone who hated his character and behavior. He also gave the back of his head a good whack on the floor. The ground was an obstacle from teleporting him over the Eiffel. As for the whirling bottle in mid-air, no heroic attempt was made at clasping that, its way was made downwards as well. It exploded into a thousand fragments upon contact with the floor. There was no more circling around. A second of dead silence passed.

"OH GOD!" cried the cleaner, his arms held out pleading, making his way towards the broken bottle and the squandered champagne. Rodric made haste in quickly scrambling to his feet as well, and Ross pursued. Rushing towards the broken bottle, images of the Eiffel Tower brightly lit in various colors skimmed through Rodric's head. And he had a long hard look at the atrocity that was laid bare on the floor. It was only after Mike grunted in an apparent attempt to divulge consideration towards his pain that everyone in the room quickly ran towards him, not as much as ran at all but rather treaded rapidly in an apparent attempt of pretending as well that they cared for him. Only Prohvark sat still with a malicious, self-satisfying smile on his face as he watched the others try to get Mike on his feet and then lay him across on the sofa. Prohvark had not expected much of the party as he thought before, but this episode had already surpassed all expectations, and he felt a sense of contentment after a long time living. "I'm okay...I'm very well alright," said Mike; however, none present had asked him. "Actually, I feel that fall has served me good. Hah, I feel restored." Then he slightly groaned again but not without trying to shroud his pain while flexing his body and stopping his hand from the urge to rub the stinging back of his head where he felt a sharp pain and every once in a while squinted his eyes because of it. It's true, in his pain, he had overlooked the destiny of the bottle, in the same way how others had neglected his fall and prioritized the breaking of the bottle.

As Mike glanced around for the first time and noticed the remnants of the bottle laying on the floor, he at once stood up with highbrowed fury and anger, forgetting all his physical pain. He was no alcoholic, but for a second, he felt exactly how they feel, forgetting all their pain with the sip of that liquid. But the liquid was wet on the floor now and dogs are not very fond of alcohol. A sudden pang to express his anger and expose it on the rest took a hold of him, to which he succumbed and obliged later on. For now, standing with scattered thoughts and an open mouth of shock, he pointed at the remnants, the cleaner taking that gesture as an order of tidying up the spot, hastily snatched his broom off the corner and got to work. "Well, there goes our trip over the Eiffel," said Rodric, in a tone that implied repressed anger and mockery pointed at Mike, who was responsible for wasting his chance of tasting the sublime champagne. Rodric looked completely dejected. He buried himself on the sofa again, Ross following the act as well. Mike shook himself from the stupor, scuttled towards the cleaner as he was disposing the bottle and what remained of it in the waste bucket. With bloodshot eyes, he stared right into the cleaner's eyes and held him tightly from both his dirty collars. At that point, he began shaking the forefinger of his left hand right beneath the cleaner's chin, spouting a few words out incoherently which no one understood. He stopped mid-sentence, apparently thinking he had said clearly enough and then he walked away to the window and lit a cigarette in his state of wrath. The scene had become a bit much humorous for Prohvark, who up till now had successfully managed to repress his laughter on a few occasions. Previously, Prohvark had noticed when the cleaner knocked on the door, there was a confident change in Mike's expression, for he earnestly thought at that moment the impossible had happened, the Boss and his assistant where at the door. But opening the door, Mikes expression changed to that of a bleak and disappointed one upon beholding the cleaner. And later, when Mike was hovering around with the champagne in his hand, Prohvark amused himself by imagining Mike was an anxious lover now delighted upon the sudden acceptance of his love letter, he started pirouetting around like a lunatic. He almost burst out laughing when Mike had fallen with a thud as if the letter brought with it rejection, but immediately slapped his knee, satisfying himself with a grin instead. The recent shaking of the finger proved till a degree far too genuine a comedy and enough for Prohvark to burst into a stream of laughter. And burst he did, so noisily that if a person walking down the street one floor below and next to the opened window, he would definitely hear the stream of laughter and think to himself, "A splendid, happy gathering must be taking place in the room above." But Mike had had enough. The last blow was dealt to his ego. The lock that held the box together was long-last broken.

"What is this INSOLENCE!" Mike approached Prohvark who was in a seated position. "How dare you? Who are you laughing at? It better be that sorry cleaner and his dirty, ragged clothes."

The latter taking that as a challenge to deny his cowardice stood up and said, "What if I was laughing at you and not the dishonest cleaner?"

"Well, what would you be laughing at me for? Is it because I fell down and made a fool out of myself? Or is it because you consider me a fool altogether, regardless of the happenings of this night?" said Mike. He almost caught Prohvark from the collars as he did the cleaner but spared him because of his profession.

"Well, what if I'm laughing at you for all the things you mentioned? Or none of it at all?" replied the breathless Prohvark.

"Well, what if you are not?"

"Well, what if I am?"

"GENTLEMEN. Stop this rigmarole right now. Let us deal with this like people, like grownups who make sense," pitched in Rodric from a corner, his voice barely audible enough so as not to disturb the state of their emotions but hoping that the argument would go further than the "What ifs?". Ross nodded in assent.

Mike began anew, still a bit drunk, "Alright. Seems to me Prohvark here has taken me to be some kind of a joke. An objhect of laughter. Especially in my downfall! The fox has come out for the night. But the fact that he laughed at me does not angerh me as much as the fact that he was repressing and hiding his laughter and contempt all the while. And the fact that he did nhot laugh at the beginning, but did so at the end, at a moment when I fell to the lowest. That is something which requires exigent consideration. For perhaps if he had laughed earlier, I would have checked myself sooner and this confrontation would not have even taken place. Who knows we could have saved the bottle as well. I blame Prohvark here foh everyone in the room missing out on that special champagne. And I blame him for my outrage as well."

"You can't be serious. And if you are serious, then you are seriously drunk enough. If your inane, silly hypothesis turns out to be true, that would mean each one of us is to blame in this room while you are just a mere victim of negligence," retorted Prohvark, "You are just angry because you have made a fool out of yourself at your own expense. There are occasions when a person who makes a fool out of himself generates pity and sympathy towards himself and gains an unexpected favorable outcome in the way he reacts to his foolishness in the aftermath. Looking at the way you have reacted, pointing your fingers and a drunk tongue at your colleagues, you have done yourself no favors at all. First, you have been a fool and later a fool drunk in presumptuousness."

"And you have no mhanners at all. How dare you, as a guest, speak to your host like that in his own house?"

"And how dare you falsely accuse your guests of whatever it is that you have accused as of. You clearly have the mighty tone of accusation on display. Also, if you want, we can take this matter outside under the night sky, then we would find ourselves freed from the roles of guest and host and whatever sense of hospitality related to it," said Prohvark sincerely, gesturing at the door.

Rodric stood up from the sofa, "Before we take this outside, how about we drink a cup, each, from the cheap bottle of whiskey? You know, merely as refreshments. Besides, a matter is much more solidly concluded and with a touch of earnestness when one is slightly tipsy. Cheers, huh!"

"NO. NO," Mike replied hastily with fervent hate and disgust, "None of you shall have anything, no more. Bheggars, the lot of you. Not worthy in my presence at all. At all. The party is hovering, hover and you all can be kind now, kind enough to yourself by leaving this very second. Every moment you stay, you expose your vile characters furthermore." He was shaking his head as he gave the orders for dispersing. But there was another not-so-pleasant surprise for Mike as he turned around and faced the table upon which he sighted the cleaner, seated with one of the whiskey bottles opened in front of him and missing about two good cups of content. The cleaner had apparently emptied the content while Mike and Prohvark argued. And now, he had the expression which conveyed he probably should have not, as Mike was approaching hurriedly towards a confrontation with him as well. The cleaner's eyes began watering up as he prepared his body language to show signs of meekness. He almost began muttering something but was cut short with a heavy blow, a burning slap to the chest by Mike.

"You are a worthless WHORM. Totally useless. You hold no value if it were not for the invention of the mhop and bucket. Take away from you that, and you won't last due to HUNGER! And imagine if people preferred dust and dirt over cleanliness. Perhaps then we could have used you, for you serve as a dirty, dusty man. Shame on you. You steal the cigarettes of hard-working employees and then get drunk in their parties on expensive bhottles of whiskey which you don't deserve." (Mike deliberately called it an expensive whiskey to intensify the feelings of guilt the cleaner felt. Or maybe he just found another opportunity to boast of his expenses and squeezed upon it. Either way, the cleaner could not possibly distinguish between what's cheap or expensive) "You showing to parties is an insult. And I feel disappointed in my judgement of inviting you. Look what you have done."

Mike would have continued berating the cleaner for a few good minutes or perhaps until the morning if not for another unexpected ring of the doorbell, which diverted the attention and gaze of all towards the door. The cleaner collapsed on the chair, completely dejected, and almost made an attempt to fill another cup to drown his utter destruction of morale.

45

6

The opened door gave sight to a fair-skinned and reasonably clean man in his early thirties of average height and a lean, precise body. A body that showed no signs of weakness and every indication of vitality at an hour sufficiently late enough for bodies to be snoozing due to exhaustion. With eyebrows thick and pointy at the edges, his face supported by a crooked nose, in those black eyes he had a look like that of a hawk, an eagle descending upon his prey. With hair thick, dark and slicked back, he was dressed in a dark black, tight-fitted and luxuriously tailored suit. A tighter suit could not be imagined without bringing to mind a man half-naked, for the suit seemed like it would lacerate on every corner upon exertion of an unseemly physical activity. Such suits were tailored for people who would conduct their daily routine without ever taking a seat. So this gentleman, the assistant of the Boss, had likely wore this suit on the occasion before exiting his apartment and walked from point A to B and C, handling his daily transactions, shaking hands with people of high stature (this fact Mike specially kept in mind when he extended his own hand for an expected rough, vigorous shaking), grinning slyly as he finalized his deals, and all this without ever taking a seat, dreading his suit might give out. Yes, you see such men who care more about the state of their suits than their stance, and for reasons comically weird enough, they usually are found holding positions that of high and mighty stature in any organization. And here, this man, this assistant had arrived like he would casually arrive on any other business-related meeting on any other busy day. For a second, he looked around as though he had landed in the wrong apartment. And he would never sit with the like of the people present in the room, even if he were wearing silk robes.

"We were just waiting for you...for you both highly esteemed, highly orderly dignitaries to arrive," screamed Mike as he rushed at the door, "The party...ceremony was on hold." He added, stretching his neck to look over and behind the shoulders of the assistant from both the sides, searching for the boss who was known to be of short stature. Mike even peeked his forehead behind but found no one else, only a butt which stood out in those pants. The assistant had arrived alone without the boss, and if the boss did accompany him, he would not be standing behind the assistant, for a view of that sight was unsettling. And Mike remembered, it is usually the case when the assistant is sent, for that means the boss is busy. They shook hands and the assistant carelessly murmured some words of congratulations. Everyone in the room was standing in respect, except Prohvark who was absentminded due to all that had happened. And Mike already had in mind to command Prohvark away from the chair, to make seat for the assistant. By such a move, Mike would have dealt Prohvark a blow of humiliation. And our protagonist would be in no position to refuse the order because that would have meant going against the assistant, his superior. But such a scene could not make it to the story, for the assistant looked around and fixed his gaze upon everyone positioned in the room as if they were pawns on a board of chess and he in power to shuffle them around. Then he slightly nodded his head in determination. Targeting a move with a fixed intention, he walked straight towards the table with the bottle of whiskey, poured it in the cup. First, he took a little sip for taste and then two whole cups in haste. After that, he turned around and walked out with the same determination by which he had arrived, without even going through the trouble of nodding at the ones present. He exited with elegance and closed the door to the apartment delicately. As the door creaked into silence, there were no words appropriate enough that could be spoken. In such a state, a few minutes passed as everyone was attempting to conjure up their thoughts, trying to make sense of what had simply happened.

There are often occasions when an individual is on course to pursue an errand, while on the course he realizes there is another issue, a secondary one, which though not important and not requiring any compulsion in fulfilling could nevertheless be of service, of remedy to himself and which so happens to be falling on the way towards the main errand. The individual then sees no harm in overtaking the fulfilment of this optional matter for his pleasure or if there is a benefit. And that is what had happened here. When the assistant was on his way towards home for a good night's sleep, which was his main priority, he had suddenly remembered the invitation of some employee who worked under him, inviting him to a promotional party. And the assistant envisioned a bottle of something present at this party that would further help him in achieving that good night's dream. So he had acted accordingly. In any case, alas, it is so and happens this way. In an event when one accomplishes a serene night, a night quiet enough to a degree that it winds up forgotten for the person for the remainder of his life, he achieves this for himself by making that same night a remorsefully unforgettable one for someone else. And if the party was not already unforgettable enough for Mike, it just became.

"Ach, if only people knew this is how promotional parties end up unfolding, perhaps then they would fear a promotion rather than craving them," said Rodric. He was getting up from the sofa, sensing the end near.

"Yes. But people know for a fact that promotion means not having to see colleagues such as you on a regular basis again. And honestly, that's the best thing about it right now," retorted Mike, on the verge of breaking down. It must be said now, if it was not already plain enough, that Mike would cling to any idea, blurting it out, if he found a sense of redeemable victory in that particular idea.

The cleaner left the apartment first, for he was closer in distance to the door than anyone else, followed by Rodric and then Ross. Prohvark looked around one last time to see Mike gazing thoughtfully at a distance out from the window. And then, a sudden revolting idea, a virtual image of tossing Mike over the window passed in his head, but it subsided as he thought there might be a passerby walking below and the falling body would cause unnecessary casualty—one stone, two bird kind of situation. Meanwhile, Rodric and Ross parted ways. But there was another incident in store for Rodric that is worthy of mentioning.

As Rodric was walking towards his apartment, contemplating the events of the party in general, he seemed genuinely pleased at how things unfolded and had grinned twice already at imagining the state of Mike left alone with the insults of the ceremony. The pavement upon which Rodric was walking was sufficiently bright, alternating streetlights and lamps were positioned evenly along the pathway. And looking across, he caught sight of the cleaner along the opposite footpath in front of him about ten feet away. The cleaner was smiling in anticipation and motioned Rodric towards a confrontation.

"Here, Sir. You dropped your packet in the afternoon today. I ran after you. But you were in hurry getting back to office and failed to take notice of me." He had clearly mistaken Rodric for Prohvark, although they were not at all similar in appearance. At the time when Mike dropped the packet, the cleaner was too excited to seize the opportunity and did so without even paying close attention to the person who had dropped it.

"Why thank you" replied Rodric, seizing the packet, not sure of what was happening. He pretended to be genuinely pleased but was surprised, more curious as to why the cleaner had decided to return the bundle, rather to whom. Rodric weighed the packet in his hand and the cleaner gave a guilty expression. He had smoked a few of them. "I could definitely use them on my way back towards home. You have made me a happy man. But you know, you could have kept them for yourself. And at no cost and intelligence I would have determined where they could have gone. In all honesty, I had already forgotten about them thinking I had consumed them already, and just now I was on my way towards purchasing another one. So could it be you have actually mended your ways after the incident with Mike. Or perhaps it's the effect of the heavily mouthed lecture he laid upon you. Or maybe you just quit smoking altogether. So, which is it?"

The cleaner gave a wry smile, he felt at ease now, with a confidence of complete assuredness at having handed the packet to its rightful owner. Why he had decided to hand it over was even troublesome for him to state, for he was a long way from being a reasonably educated man and his command of the verbally expressed language, the only one he could speak, his native tongue, was of a powerless state as well. His vocabulary was not something to admire. Nevertheless, he chose to convey his sentiments and spend a minute on the spot looking for the right words to decipher his emotions. He was one of those people who could not distinguish between two men, as the incident made it evident, but who rightfully claimed they found the one and only true god. And so he began blabbering to the best of his abilities.

"Well. Sir. You see. I returned them on an account of redeeming that godforsaken man up there. The one promoted."

"Redeem? Mike?" said Rodric with confusion.

"Yes. Indeed. I thought to myself. There might not be a single happy man that is happy or in a happy state because of the actions and character of that man up there. So I took it upon myself. To act righteously on account of him. You see. So perhaps God might forgive him. And if that man up there were to die now, all out of a sudden, then he has left something which is worthy of him having a case in his pleadings in the afterlife. And all thanks to my generosity. Me. Whom he called an insect! I put it on myself to act rightly on his lecture, so he could be given a part of the good deed as well," the cleaner spoke with contorted eyebrows, shaking his head from time to time.

"Ha! I'm not sure of the message that you are attempting to send. Could it be that you are forcing God into forgiving a man? The way you put it seems like an old case of blackmail and extortion!"

"Oh, NO. No. Nonono. God forbid, Sir. No. Could be the other way around. It could be that god has forced me to act on his lecture and quit smoking and look for the one who lost his packet of cigarette and return them, so god can give Mike a chance. God forbid. God knows. But I have forgiven that unhappy man over there. That's the beauty of forgiveness. It can be given. Handed out. Without arms being stretched towards it. Such beauty. Man who committed wrong and evil. Man who called me a worm, without batting an eye, with no remorse or repentance, exactly like I was one. That such arrogant man can still be forgiven by their victims, alone in the company of their dark rooms on late hours, when they go again, all over, through the suffering of what they have been put through, slain through, in their corners. And they end up by forgiving with tears falling from their eyes, yes, Sir, tears. That same worm. While expecting no repentance. Sir."

The cleaner was shaking in sobs and twice he did wipe the tears rolling down his wrinkly cheeks. Rodric, knowing not how to respond, was caught in a puzzle whether to let him proceed or to stop him by consolation. And in his growing confusion, he tried handing back the packet of cigarettes, similar to the manner how babies are given desserts to stop their whining. The cleaner was evidently ruffled at this. Grabbing his brush and bucket, he walked away furiously. Rodric, with shoulders shrugged and a wave of his hand, lit up a cigarette, dismissed the whole incident, and went his way to wherever he was headed.

A while later, as Prohvark took his road alone upon which he also spotted the cleaner across the opposite direction. The latter spotted the first with a smile and then a puzzled look that gradually transformed itself into such an expression of shock that seemed to imply as if someone had seen god. While in truth, it was only an expression of having discovered that something which was lost had been returned to the wrong hands. The cleaner quickened his pace upon this realization and treaded back across the direction from which he was initially approaching towards our protagonist. Possibly, he went back looking for Rodric, thinking to himself what a waste of good cigarettes he had let go off, given away from his own hands. And musing over the ways of god. In such musings, a person might find god but will for sure forget the way which led him to the discovery. So, the cleaner in confusion had lost his way, and forgetting the path which he came from went on a different direction. Prohvark noticed the various changes in the demeanor of the cleaner walking away, and he himself shrugged his shoulder and with a wave of his hand dismissed the incident similar to how Rodric had done a while earlier.

The streets were silent. It was that time after midnight when everyone was either sleeping soundly or awake in tormenting thoughts. But Prohvark fell amongst neither of those two. He walked peacefully, consumed by a feeling of contentment, wishing that this specific night and the calm, silent atmosphere associated with it must remain forever. If only he could walk till the end without the sun rising in the morning again and along with it all the people. He looked at the sky which began to seem wonderful now, only due to his inner state of being. Although there were only a few sparkling stars, Prohvark assured himself that the sky on this particular night was as flawless as it could be. And he told himself any single addition of a star would spoil its beauty. Gazing at the sky every once in a while and then looking at the lamppost which lit the street, he certainly saw some familiarities. But the sky appeared totally free of human control which led to its structural beauty, while the lights along the street were restricted by the designs and limitations of the creative potential of the human mind. Prohvark began painting a mental picture of the sky lit up by the streetlights and the streets lit up by the stars in the sky. And he felt completely sure if in any way such a miracle was to fall upon this world, then the stars would fall to precisely only light places on earth that was the most deserving of them all and would completely transform that specific place into such a beauty that it would become a place of worship and veneration not only for human beings but for every species in the world. While in the opposite scenario, the post lights from the streets would be all over the place in a state of turmoil across the sky, adding nothing to its tremendous magnificence while also failing to take anything away from it. Amidst those thoughts, a question represented itself: whether the people he was involved with that evening found themselves under the same sky as well? And before the answer arose, Prohvark found himself at the doorstep of his apartment. Without a moment's delay, he hastened towards opening the door, buried himself on the bed, his heavy body sinking in the cushions that seemed particularly soft and comforting than they ever did on any other day. After a series of surprises that tired people out, what else could come next if not the familiar steps of sleep approaching fast yet setting in stealthily. And after such a sleep, hopefully not a nightmare.

7

In the early afternoon, when the sun was occasionally creeping in through the curtains, its rays falling directly on our protagonist's fatigued, resting face and when little birds sitting on the edge by the window were chirping in a sharp and shrilling manner, our protagonist could not be shaken from his slumber. And while there he lay and snorted noisily and uncomfortably, which implied the possibility of an awful sleep, a minute must be taken to describe the facial attributes that were overlooked so far, somehow, of this human being, the legend of our story who lately had forgotten how to be.

Laying on his back on the bed, straight and extended completely, one could say that Prohvark was of the average height, neither short nor long but having spent time around individuals who were comparatively short in stature, he gave in to believing that he was longer than the average male. And it did seem like that to the eye if he was laying on the bed. But if he was to lay on the ground and the distance of his sleeping body was to increase from the eye, then maybe a person would say that he was a bit shorter than the average male. The second toes of both his legs were longer than the first one, and every day before crowning his legs with shoes, he would foolishly pull the main toe with an abysmal strength, hoping to level them out over time. Yes, our protagonist was rational when it came to maintaining the symmetry of his physical structure. Blessed with a fair complexion, the type which would unfortunately change colors to often uncover his inner emotions too clearly, winding up as a curse for someone who constantly tried to maintain his privacy, for example, our protagonist. What could be said about his nose? Only that when a fly would sit upon it, and Prohvark, in an attempt to shoo the fly away, would end up grazing his nose with the tip of his fingers, the sensation of touch, served as a reminder of constantly undermining its long protruding length. And when that same fly buzzed around his ears, it felt the temptation of feasting upon the abundance of earwax, which could frequently be seen around the ears of our hero because of his neglect in cleaning that region. The reality of having an excess of wax inside his perfectly round and semi-circled ears didn't do justice at all to another fact, which was, in actuality the hard work and the time he spent in attempting to groom himself and maintaining his toilet. The reason for the wax was its placement, which at a first glance to his naked eye fell under invisibility and the fact that our hero was always in a hurry, resulting in neglect only due to forgetfulness. Likewise, it must be stated that there are certain other areas of the human body which share the similarities of being in a troublesome position and invisible as well to the naked eye just like the dark insides of the ear. But to say that our saint, the legend of our story, failed in cleaning those parts as well would be painting a terribly bad image of him leading to an insult, and since Prohvark doesn't take lightly to possible insults, it's better to avoid delving into such subtleties. His eyes, moulded as a perfect oval, the color dark brown, a color revealed under direct sunlight, were mostly taken to be black and it gave the impression of the spirit being in a careless state of reverie someplace far away, far from current reality, unless aroused. One can see the world, or even the universe in an individual's eyes, but Prohvark's world didn't amount to much. The eyes were shaded by long, dim eyelashes. Honestly, it can be said that the eyes were the only feature that provided a trace of beauty and an intrigue for captivation in an otherwise lacklustre and plump face. Much has already been said about the eyes of our delicate hero, but if a stranger was to eye our protagonist walking down the street with a delicate eye, the stranger would surely conclude upon inspecting his body that it fell under the category of somewhat being overweight. And if the stranger was a gym instructor guiding for a fee, he would surely try and urge Prohvark to take a couple of classes under him, whereupon our hero would take a breath in and drive his stomach inwards, flattening it out in an attempt to make himself look thin before a quick and outright refusal, walking away briskly. His right hand swaying more than his left, he would pat his stomach with a grin indicating his pride at having a chubby tummy. Once it happened, two boys pointed at him laughing, and of them, the rosy one announced, "If that person ova'deyr was to ride a donkey, the donkey would shuwarly ask foh'sum assistance from his fellow companion donkeys." Prohvark convoluted and answered, "I suppose you simply made a reference ova'deyr to the incompetence of you and your sidekick!" As he said this, his upper lip, which was slightly narrower than the lower, parted upwards revealing the white of his teeth and a part of his tongue. Now a minute has already passed and enough has been said about the physical qualities of a person in a story, a story wherein physique doesn't matter and in which there is no guide really towards attaining the kind of body favored by society.

Prohvark awoke by the noise of a crow cawing non-stop and annoyingly. A bunch of crows. Opening his eyes, the first thing he spotted was the culprits behind the window. The crow spread its wings for a flight in haste and a few feathers tumbled off them as it vanished out of sight. In the free and open sky, the crow seemed to direct his flight, making his way towards a specific destination to fly towards. Prohvark walked towards the window and pulled aside the plain white muslin curtains, the daylight fell through the window and upon the table only, while the chairs kept around the table were still to some degree covered in the same dull light as the whole room was.

He sat down on a chair. He was frightened at having caught sight of a foreign object kept under his pillow upon which he was just sleeping. The object, yellow in color, was sticking out from under the pillow by about 4 inches. And Prohvark tried to imagine having something in his possession of a yellow color, but without mistake, he did not. It was clear that he never stuffed anything under his pillow as well. So he moved towards the object with anxiety, thinking that someone, a thief or an outsider could have been rummaging around in his apartment the night he was at the party. The thief enjoying his time alone with all that he could steal, much more than Prohvark enjoyed his time at the party. He set aside the possibility of it being a thief as there was nothing that seemed to have been stolen. Then he realized that there was nothing of value in the apartment anyway that was worth stealing, and it might be that the thief after scrounging for hours to find something and becoming gravely disappointed at having found nothing had devised a certain plan to exact revenge on whoever was residing in his mind in this godforsaken dreadfully dull place. Or maybe the whoever had barged in was looking for a confrontation with Prohvark. However it was, Prohvark hauled out the object from under the pillow instead of displacing it and it turned out to be an envelope, sealed by a black sticker. He had never received any letters by post, nor did any mailman ever mistakenly ring on his doorbell, thinking it to be the address of some delivery. So he knew with a sense of fear that the envelope was placed there on purpose. He placed the envelope on the table and quickly ran in the toilet, splashing his face with water and wiping it off with a towel. Then he placed himself on a chair and gazed at the envelope for a couple few moments. Under the sunlight, the envelope was shining a little and seemed to have been packaged with such a caution that implied whoever had managed to pack it had a gun kept on his head which told him he only had a single attempt to perfect it. With a dry throat, Prohvark stripped off the sticker, looked around the room and back at the envelope. He took out the paper which was folded into three. He did not have to unfold it to understand that there was some sort of a message, a letter, because the ink used in writing was darkly thick enough to be seen from two sides of the paper. Furthermore, the smell of the ink raced through his nostrils and hit the 'Detective' part of his brain. Noisily, he said to himself, "Appears to just have been composed recently." He unfolded the paper slowly and extended it from both ends, then he laid a careful eye on it.

The writings were in the style of bold cursive letters and each word ended with a flare. The entire piece had a peculiarity which made it resemble an official letter, and Prohvark felt he was by all accounts not the only individual to have received this envelope. Indeed, even the contents of the message made it clearer that the envelope had been distributed to a number of people at the same time and since the beginning of it. The same words constructed in the same style. Each like the other. It was written in such a precise manner as if being written by the hands who had held the same pen a thousand times. The pen, like a sword passing on from one dying hand to the next, drawing the intensity of life and growing stronger from each hand which had fallen dead. Prohvark's tongue, which was sheathed up until now, began to twist in preparation for the exercise of reading. He also swallowed a bit of saliva and pricked his ears, then tapped his cheeks twice on both sides. He scratched his knee for a good three seconds while having violent intentions towards the mosquito who had feasted upon him, and then with a gentleness, he patted the spot which was bitten as though at last reconciling with the criminal who had chomped him and done him harm. Prohvark forgave the mosquito, but his knee was still itching. Yet he began to read, and as he read, the itch quickly subsided into forgetfulness. Finally, the letter, or the scroll as one might call it and or the creed another, read as follows:

WE HAVE KNOWN YOUR PLIGHT.

THE PLIGHT OF YOURS WAS CONTAINED IN PEOPLE WHO EXISTED BEFORE YOU. AND WE KNOW THAT SAME PLIGHT IS CONTAINED IN PEOPLE OF PRESENT.

WHEN THEY TRIED, THEY FAILED TO FIND THE MEANS OF ESCAPE. FURTHER, THE WALLS WERE CORNERING IN ON THEM AS THEY TRIED WITH A SENSE OF URGENCY. THE HANDS OF POWER PRESSURED THEM AND THEY LOST THEMSELVES LIKE CHILDREN. UNAWARE OF THEIR SITUATION, NOT WANTING THAT SITUATION.

THE PLIGHTED WERE DIVIDED WITH SUBTLE AND KEEN INSTRUMENTS SO AS TO NOT ACCUMULATE THE FORCE OF PLIGHT WHICH COULD HAVE CAUSED A POTENTIAL CHAOS BY RIOT. THE BALLOON FILLED WITH EXCESSIVE AIR IS IN ROUTE TOWARDS A THIRST FOR BURSTING. WE HAVE OFFERED AN ESCAPE, SINCE ESCAPE WAS ORDAINED AS A CHOICE. AND WE PROVIDE THAT CHOICE TO YOU NOW. FOR WE FIND YOU WORTHY OF OVERTAKING ORDAINMENT. VISIT US WITHIN A DAY OF READING THIS MANUSCRIPT OR ELSE THE WAY OF ENTRY WILL BE CLOSED. REMEMBER, WE KNOW WHEN A DAY HAS ELAPSED AND WE CAN SEE YOU WHILE YOU READ THIS LETTER AND WHEN YOU HAVE READ IT. FOLLOW THE INSTRUCTIONS TO GAIN ACCESS TO THE SECRET UNDERGROUND WORLD THAT WE HAVE CONSTRUCTED...

The remainder of the letter contained those guidelines of access, which were printed in a different format compared with the beginning of the letter. As Prohvark sat there having done reading the letter, he found himself to be a victim of only a certain kind of plight related to his professional life, which he felt morosely on a daily basis. It was obvious to him that was the only plight he needed to escape from, and the escape was being offered in the letter. On occasions too many, an individual subconsciously refuses to abolish the last obstacle that stops him from leading a different existence. While if there were obstacles a many, he would undertake to abolish one of them. This frame of mind is often adapted by people who cannot manage to fathom a life different to what they have led, regardless of it appearing brighter. While there are people who refuse to destroy the last obstacle, there are also people on the other side of a similar extreme who refuse to walk out of the last door remaining. And there are others, who will create an obstacle by themselves. Maybe they will throw banana peel on the entry towards a new life. And then cultivate inside them a fear of slipping on that peel. So it's frequently by choice that people remain in a situation of distress. So what if a life is full with tears? They tell themselves. I know where the tears stream from. So what if a life is in repetition? At least I know where the circle ends. So saying to themselves they are under the illusions of comfort. Right about on the brink of hating the chains that hold them horribly for so long, almost at the brink of the last action that could turn out to be the destroyer of that painful chain, they instead take a quick U-turn and suffice themselves to look upon that chain with an eye of familiar loveliness. This is what the misuse of a positive outlook while making the most of one's current situation often leads to. A rat cannot in a rat trap think and comfort himself by saying at least I have got an island as a view from this cage. Prohvark's curiosity about the envelope and the secret underground was barely aroused. He left his apartment for a stroll in order to shackle his thoughts a little bit here and a tittle bit there.

There was once a farmer who happened to have the fortune of winning a million in lottery. But his mind was still occupied by trifles. Thoughts swam across the vast space in his head, a space infinitely larger than the only acre of land he owned and was completely occupied by that land alone. What if there was a patch of foul crops? What if a cow was to get sick and die? What if the weather turned out to be unmerciful? And what of the millions he had just won? In a similar state, our protagonist was possessed while taking his stroll. Although to directly call him a farmer would be a mistake. In no way is his physique fit enough to be that of a farmer. One look at his overgrown stomach, and all such suspicions are dissolved.

8

By the time Prohvark was almost tired of strolling around, he came across a billiard club. He went down the stairs that led to the club's door. Once inside the club's premises, he ordered a tea and sat in a sturdy chair against the handles of which his plump tummy rested perfectly. The waiter swiftly brought in his cup of tea which was prepared beforehand and stored in a heat-retaining container. After handing the tea, the waiter stood around with a bowed head and a smile which often reveals the pride of having done a job successfully and then demanding a reward, a tip. Looking at the waiter, Prohvark took a sip of tea, slurped it and began to look around obliviously. The waiter returned with an empty hand and an overall grim outlook towards his occupation. The club contained a few visitors, but the place seemed deserted due to its size being fairly huge. An old man occupied a chair, his face flushed and his drunk head was drooping downwards in dejection, jerking once every now and then. His overgrown beard would brush against the table upon which he was leaning. He was grunting and demanded another glass of cold whiskey. But they deemed him unstable, and his order was refused in order to maintain the civility and atmosphere of the club. The old man seemed like a usual visitor of the club.

A game of pool was played by two young individuals,

students belonging to a university that did not care whether such students attend classes or not. The rail of lights over the billiards table fell dimly on their faces. As they would circle around the rectangular table, the light shadowed their faces in various ways, changing the expressions on their look. Sometimes revealing a part, emphasizing it much more than the rest. The light would cast a shadow of one's nose on the cheek, which would make the other think, "Oh, I never noticed. But he has rather a long nose." And sometimes the light would completely shadow, put in darkness the other's eye and the skin surrounding it, giving him a sinister look, which would also veil his expression of how sure he was about the shot going in? Doubtful? Confident or over? While sometimes one of them, in order to cover the amateurism of their shots, would just blame the lighting.

One of them had the air and demeanor of playing victoriously while the other was constantly making an effort to match the skill of the other. It was the turn of one making the effort to try and tuck the ball in. After a shot which was attempted with focus and a strong determination, the clutter of balls sounded and the young man slapped his thigh in frustration of failure. While the other chalked his stick planning his next shot. Another student who had just walked in joined them, as friends in a group without invitation do. Dragging a chair noisily, he sat by the table. A conversation ensued amongst them. Their sound was barely audible to our protagonist, but once he pricked those ears, there was no escaping them. Indeed, only a pricking was needed to overhear them. And sipping tea was needed to enjoy.

The tallest of them with broad shoulders who was playing victoriously spoke in a ruffled voice, "Did you read the news today, about the goat?"

"Yeah," replied the thin student with spectacles who was losing shamefacedly and glad that an opportunity of conversation ensued so attention could partially be taken away from his situation. He pounced upon the topic in a manner which implied he was more than willing to elongate it and take it on until the game was over. "Even goats have fallen a victim to the decadence of the contemporary society. What an evil act to commit. That too upon a goat in pregnancy. And it would be understandable if it was a single man who had done this vulgar act, drunk in his stupor. But a group of eight individuals?" here he shook his finger as if gesturing to some other person involved.

"Yes. Yes," said the student who had just arrived, with a careless voice of indifference, "It almost seems like the whole thing was planned beforehand. The way businessmen hold meetings right before determining who must hold shares and how much of it in the company. Here too, the victim seemed to have been carefully selected. And the day as well. And although they were found to be drugged while in the act of violation. It just, it seems that...umm...they were in a normal, sober state of mind that is if a meeting did actually take place. For the way the whole debacle had been planned implied their sobriety. But only crazy minds, intoxicated or not, would even think of acting in such a way."

"What a vile thing to do," said the broad-shouldered one as he lined up another shot which was bound to go in, "A vile thing. And they killed her too, after they had washed their hands. They made her a scapegoat for their pent-up emotions. A scapegoat."

"Hmm, hmm. A sacrificial lamb. Except this goat was not a lamb but a fully grown one. As is evident that it was pregnant, for lambs biologically can't conceive children. Ahrmm, I mean they can't conceive other goats. Or baby lambs. Whatever you get the point, until they reach a certain age."

"And the culprits? have they been arrested?"

"Yes, they have been," said the losing voice, "But not all of them. They are claiming they were persuaded by a leader, who is yet to be arrested. A so-called mastermind. Who himself did not partake in the act but led them to it, overseeing that every small detail be executed according to the requirements. And they say they were merely sheep of a shepherd. So technically, there was no crime involved on their part, they claim innocence, proclaiming that sheep and goats are known to mate together. So the search is on for the charismatic leader who acted as a shepherd leading the herd. The arrested claim they were in a trance throughout the beginning until it all ended. And they have been investigated individually. All share the same story."

"Hmm, a very complicated case," said the seated one, "All sense is lost. First, a goat is made the scapegoat. And now, they are trying to put it all on just a single person. And what should the punishment be for such lot? The punishment for murder of a human being is quite known. But the murder of a goat? One which is in pregnancy. There are also talks of another case recently. Men acquitted, three of them from the charges of harassment and abuse because it was said the woman, the victim, did not fight back or resist. Viewing the footage. However, the footage does not really capture human emotions. So who is to say, perhaps the women saw the futility in trying to fight back against the physical power of the three overgrown man. So she must have just sat there in a total acceptance of the fact that men mostly have an advantage when it comes to physical attributes, and with such a reality of a hell burning within her, it could have made her appear cold on the outside. True, they say justice is blind, and if it is so, then a pair of artificial eyes won't be of any help to it at all. Anyway, so in this case, how can a goat, as well, I mean can a goat resist? So umm, how do we go about this case?"

The spectacled student sat on the edge of table in such a position that the other who was setting up a shot could not make a claim of hindrance to his play. He began speaking, "Well, I have a friend who is a student of law. After an attempt at dissecting the case left and right, he has come to the conclusion that they could be charged for unlawful barbarity. I said the case is quite complicated to be labelled as such. It could go as a mental disorder. A manic episode. For it must be said that it was an act devoid of complete sense. Craziness. And nobody wants to be labelled crazy. Hence, nobody will perceive of going down that path again. But I am not a student of law. You see, the goat was buried. Oh what a funeral they made out of that. A whole group of people arose treating the dead goat with the sentiments equaling to that of a martyr. And I dare say, not even a king's horse. A king's! A conqueror's, who rode around on it while slaying his enemies across the land, looting their houses. Not even such a horse was gifted with the kind of a grand funeral that our goat was bestowed upon."

"I would go as far saying not even the king's daughter. His own daughter's funeral for that matter, not his stepdaughter. I just had to clarify, you know, for kings, they are known to have a lot of steps here and there. Much more steps there are in relation to them than the steps that lead to their mansion's door," said the seated one who had arrived late. Every time he spoke, he would gaze at the balls rolling around the table. If a ball was pocketed, exactly at that point he would also find a way to conclude his sentence. And his tone would drop as well.

"Yes. Yes. But such a funeral. By God! Such a crowd. They showered the coffin with such flowers that you only see nowadays in the deep forest. I swear, such splendid flowers if bought for you, with glittering eyes you would stare at them, probably suspecting them as being artificial. A middle-aged man, or rather was he old, it is not known precisely. But one of them snatched a flower from the coffin's lid just so he could take it back home to impress his wife."

"By heavens! They also say a group amongst that crowd slayed a cow specially for the occasion and brought its meat for offering at the altar. But a commotion arose since the rest claimed that the goat was a vegan while it lived. They were nearly at blows. So the offerings were rejected. Ah, to what goal does progress lead a man. I say the cup of knowledge has been filled to the verge and filling it furthermore is an exercise in futility. I say knowledge and progress has its breaking point, which once if crossed, could be detrimental to its own self. And I believe that's why a constant effort is being maintained to maim people and to dumb them down in order to shield that limit and to keep the water from overflowing. I believe that once the cup of knowledge is filled to its brink, it must be immediately consumed and made empty again. Empty, so it can be filled over and again. Possibly until we have changed the cup. The container. An improved, enhanced one. I believe a very high caution must be taken to stop the substance of the cup from flooding. I believe..." God only knows what else the one who had just been winning, victorious at the game, would have kept on believing, if not for the old man at the table grunting uproariously, which diverted all of their attention towards him for a second but unfortunately led to the conversation resuming back on track.

In our world, it so happens that when a man becomes successful in a minor event of his life, even if it's by luck, he starts to have faith and believe in almost everything. So if he has had luck at let's say renting cars, then he would think of himself as a mechanical engineer of vehicles and of airplanes as well. To such a degree, the confidence of the individual who had just won only a game of billiards arose, and in a moment, he began to think of himself as a specialist in logic, an expert philosopher. But a great swimmer barely makes it as an average surfer. And one who wins a billiard game cannot even kick the soccer ball. But unfortunately for us and for our ears, that doesn't stop him from voicing his opinion. Such a trait, ultimately, acts as a drawback, an impediment and is destructive for the one who is in possession of it. For he might attract only people foolish enough as an audience for his illusion of expertise. While the ones who know and understand will deviate from his path, finding him annoying. The ones with wisdom who could have been of benefit to the person with the flawed trait are deprived from also visiting him in order to learn something or for an advice in regard to the original profession in which the said person had found success initially. It certainly stopped our protagonist from joining the victorious broad-shouldered one at the pool table.

"Indeed, however, the incident did not end there. Days later, the grave was found to be uncovered and the corpse was all found but missing. There upon began the bits of gossip that the leader of the arrested group was at work here. But the group whose offerings were rejected claimed that it was a terrible omen for having denied their offerings of the cow. Never mind the groups. The arrested say the plan was to cook the goat and serve it to the needy and the poor. Furthermore, they are also claiming a group such as theirs is on the rise in places around the world. So this case is bound to be repeated, or who knows perhaps this isn't even the first and the others have just not been caught in the act yet."

"Strange times. This...But what do the captured say in regard to conducting those rituals? The goal...what's the superstition behind it? Although it seems to be possible that if such a calumny was contrived again, there at least a spectacle will not arise in regard to the scene which happened at the burial service. Or any of those foolish groups involved. For people would have adjusted their faculties to it. Chaos leads to more chaos at first, but gradually some sense begins to be extracted from it. Always has been that way."

"Indeed. Definitely! Well said." They were just cheering on each other so they could continue with the topic. "All things considered and moving on, the authorities are reluctant to share that part of information. They are claiming the suspects have no specific purpose. Saying it was a moment of desperation and they were possessed by the passions of lust, under the influence of drugs and all that pent-up energy. But it's undeniable that they are concealing something. And if they are hiding the reason for those rituals, it must mean the reason could, in their opinion, lead more people towards the contemptible ritual, popularizing the cult to a stage of rampancy. Gradually, the number of followers might increase. The pioneer of this group is said to be wondering around, searching for more followers, urging random people to partake in the ritual so they can see with their own eyes whether it yields results after completion."

"What nonsense. What filth," cried the spectacled one who had lost, as he threw the stick which rolled towards the end of the table, "Well then, tomorrow, I can create any superstition that I please while urging the people to act in a particular way in order to make it come true." The spectacled loser was actually not in the least bit interested in the topic. He was just hiding behind it so he could mask his failure at playing billiards. He was ashamed.

"You see that's exactly why they should not simply detain them for unlawful barbarity," said the victorious one, now also a part-time criminologist, thanks to his victory, as he leaned against the table. A couple of more victories at billiards and God forbid, he might set up his own detective shop. "They have to slap this incident with some notion of a mental disorder attached to it. And they have to prove that the superstition lacked any real merit. No legitimacy, so as to say it's crazy. It's madness. Only then people can stop going down that chaotic rabbit hole. This is not a case where one person has committed an act that transgresses the laws of nature. But a group of people, guided by a superstition and a belief, not just by lust, for all we know they might have been straight individuals and put even themselves through the torment of...let's just say doing it with the goat... so as to accomplish the end of the ritual. It is possible the drugs were consumed to make the ordeal easier for themselves. Again, there were eight people, and it's more likely that those people were gathered first and then told about the subtleties of the activity and not gathered beforehand based on their sexual preferences because it would be very hard to detect people who share this specific kind of preference in sexuality, for they keep it a secret since it is shunned by society. Likewise, how on earth is a person to go around and question people without raising suspicions towards himself as well! There are various other reasons to the difficulty of assembling such a group. In short, these eight people were brought together at random and persuaded by a reward."

"True. Facts. Only facts. Coincidentally, there is another outstanding rumor that has quite recently begun to spring in time with this occasion. A secret weapon that the powerful have manufactured, which can recognize a person's sexual preferences by monitoring his heartbeat and brain activities. An experiment was conducted to test the credibility of the weapon in which a human was to stare at another, first of the similar gender and then the opposite. After several moments, it would yield successful results, ten times out of ten. But there was a noteworthy drawback discovered while they took the experiment to another level by including an animal. No, the test was not conducted upon a rat as you gentleman are suspecting. A wedded man of around thirty years volunteered to partake in the experiment, only for the sake of the advancement of science. A female canine was put in front of him to stare at. The outcome confused everyone. And why is that? What do you think happened? At first, the results were clear. But after a while of repetition, after the married man was made to stare for a while longer than appropriate, the results began to shift. There were certain desires of lust beginning to spring in his head. And the machine gave positive readings. The only conclusion they derived at the end, which was a philosophical one rather than being scientific, was the conclusion that everything can be morphed and regarded as a sexual object of appeasement to the animal mind, particularly the male, if the eyes of such a mind were to contemplate and tread with dread around the edges of those desires, minutes longer than required. Even a white wall. It also proved true when the experiments were conducted towards inanimate objects as well. And what about the married man? Well, he was kept under secret surveillance for a while, but they gave up after no signs of suspicious activities. And the poor guy's marriage almost ended up as divorce. The entire neighborhood caught wind of the experiment and the man's reputation was tarnished. The gossip among the in-laws and other relatives began. Some of them said they knew there was something off about him. That was until they asked the wife to partake in the experiment as well. Which straightened up, patched things out and made them equal."

"Yeah, they say he was followed around to see whether he would purchase any watermelons, despite the fact it was towards a canine that the deviations occurred. Nevertheless, an odd experiment. That's science in a nutshell, more or less. It proves that a human being is capable of falling under two extremes. That's all. But he falls under one extreme at a particular time and ricochets to the next in a matter of seconds. By what machine do you explain that? Regardless of there being a machine or a so-called experiment that could detect the reason, in order to stop the bounce from happening, it would scarcely be of any use, for the reason is also a subject of constant change. Anyway, does the group only target goats that are repugnant? Pardon me, pregnant?!"

Prohvark reclined on his chair and shifted his attention away from the conversation and upon his tea. After taking a sip, he found to his dismay, it had gone completely cold. The conversation at the table was still hotly going on, but there was no one around to focus upon it. Now it was finally reduced to a murmur that all sounded, deservedly, like rubbish. There are certain topics that only make sense when the focus is no longer laid upon it. And it's for our benefit that we must neglect those topics and be wise enough to stop ourselves from discussing them. Of what benefit is a discourse about goats in the event that it isn't done in respect to the farming and agricultural life. Or making a steak out of it. Or when it becomes a painful discussion for vegetarians. It's all merely grazing at that point.

The old man who had been demanding for more drinks to no avail and was grunting and jerking, now laid motionless with his head upon the table. Prohvark walked towards him with the cold cup of tea in his hand. He nudged the old man so as to offer him the tea, which was for himself no longer drinkable. He nudged him again and patted his back. The old man after lifting his head up shook his head strongly and with such a vigor as if without doing that, it would unscrew and fall away from his shoulders, becoming just a ball that the generation of youth would knock in towards the pocket of the billiards table, all the while claiming victory at having done so. And if the youth talked so high and confidently when they pocketed a normal ball of pool, the reader can imagine the level of their confidence when they do so with a human head. Confidence level over nine thousand maybe.

"Ahhh...goaatss...ehh...whayss the group of whiskey?" the old man grunted. He wished to be loud, but all he could summon with his energy was a forceful grunt, a sound which seemed to be generating within his stomach, and by the time it travelled upwards through all the organs, finally escaping from the mouth, it was beaten out of all its energy and reduced to a sound of insignificance. The cup which he had emptied thrice was still kept on the table, the waiter not having done his job enthusiastically this time by taking them away. Probably he had been thinking, "If the young fellow who was fully aware and maintained his senses..." (obviously not being aware of the fact that our protagonist usually talks to himself like a schizophrenic) "if that young man won't tip me for my diligence in working, then there is not a farthing of a chance that this old man, drunk and out of his faculties would give me anything also." So thinking, he let the cup remain on the table. Such is the story of that cup's situation, which the old man now grasped in his hand, and not being in his right mind to detect the difference in the weight of a full cup and an empty one, he peered into it expecting it might contain something. But all it contained was a reeking smell of what had already reached the bladder of the old man by now. Prohvark handed the old man his cold cup of tea. The old man grinned delicately, his eyes gleamed like the eyes of a father whose son after serving in a war has just arrived home with medals of honor. And whose arrival they would celebrate with party and drinks. Hopefully unlike the one which our protagonist went through.

"Thank you. Betta late thay nevar," he said, mistaking Prohvark for the waiter.

Prohvark began to make his exit and was at the door of the club with the stairs ascending to the streets lit by a splendid sun. Paying no attention to the grunting of the old man that were ignited once again, he began to walk away.

"WHAA…I asked fo whisk…not col tea…yo no gettin any tips from MEH! Come bac heya!" snorted the old man. Getting no response, he pulled the empty cup that was stinking of whiskey. Now he was dejected, perhaps like a father who hears the news that his son might never come from the war. And with that no arrival party. So he poured whatever remained of the cold tea into the vacant cup which previously held the whiskey in order to scavenge whatever of the whiskey was stuck to the inner walls or at least for the tea to end up smelling like it to suffice his addictive thirst. Immersing two fingers halfway inside the liquid, he began stirring it, not in perfectly circular motions but hitting the insides of the cup, jolting it around which led to a little bit of the tea spilling over and onto the table. Then he bought his hand towards his mouth with those two fingers sticking out of it while tiny drops of tea dripped off from them and back into the cup. Moving his head forward, he wrapped his lips around the two fingers, as if demonstrating how a depressed person was likely to shoot himself through the mouth. Licking them dry before gulping the tea blend down his throat, his head fell, and he dozed away with his head and arms all over the table. Two fingers still stack out of his right hand, making the gesture of the peace sign, as the conversation at the table went on in the background amongst the college students, however, most likely towards another topic.

9

Next morning, Prohvark woke up at 7:30 in the morning. He mechanically began preparing to dress up for his work at the office. Oh, how the shirt slipped through his arms and his tie pressed against his neck and how everyday he wished that he had still been laying on his bed with nothing but an underwear. As he combed his hair into a form that fell under accepted civility, he relished the population who went bald at an early age. But he failed to completely put himself in the shoes of a bald man, for they had troubles of their own, such as how to powder their head to minimize the sparkle and the amount of light it reflected. "Why they must not have to go through the hassle of perfecting their hairstyle. What a nuisance those strands now and again turn out to be. The strands, they stand as rebels do against conformity, each crying out with an existence of its own. 'I shall not bend and I shall not soften,' they seem to be saying. What precisely do they rebel against?" So thought our protagonist and he thought out loud, as he maintained a steady battle, a conflict of putting those strands back under the flock where they belonged. He brushed them twice and over again, yet the strand stayed solid. Prohvark realized that this was a strand of stubborn nature, so he licked his palm as a weapon and licked it again. He raised his palm and squashed the strand against his head and began scouring it vigorously. Meanwhile, he imagined to himself that the strand was frothing, begging for mercy but instead of pity, a smile of subtle enjoyment in cruelty spread across his plump cheeks. He kept on rubbing the spot upon which the strand had decided to prosper as he made his way towards the mirror in the toilet. Finally observing himself in the mirror, he decided that it was sufficient amount of torture and stopped rubbing his palm against the powerless strand of hair. Standing still with his hand laid across the top of his head, he looked at himself in the mirror as his expression changed because he had just remembered the letter, the manuscript he had received yesterday. Exiting the toilet, he went back to the table upon which the letter was kept. It was still kept precisely in the same position as he had left it yesterday. So he quickly read it all over once again, with his hand still taming the top corner of his head where the solitary strand of defiant hair had constructed its abode. He paid special attention towards the part in which instructions for accessing the entrance were jotted down. After having done reading it hastily, he went back to the mirror in order to examine the victim he had flattened out. He began to raise his hand slowly, as one does when they are opening a box of gift that was being anticipated for quite a while. Slightly tilting his head towards the right, the sight of battle became visible to him, and Prohvark triumphantly saw his foe, the strands of hair slain down below, next to the rest. Slightly polished and shinier than the rest due to the saliva used in greasing it into position. Prohvark carried the hand with which he had roughened the hair up towards his nose and sniffed it like someone who was addicted, then he gesticulated like a commander and exclaimed unmistakably to himself in the mirror, "I love the smell of saliva in the morning, it smells like...victory!" He quickly looked at the envelope one last time before making his way towards the apartment door with a look in his eyes of having not forgotten it. As he slammed the door behind him, the air generated by the force of the slam resurrected the strand of hair back into existence, symbolizing: in war, the only victory is survival.

Prohvark had not yet conclusively settled on the idea of following the crystal-clear instructions on opening the path that led to the underground place where he was welcomed. He remained unsure, partly because there was a vague sense floating in his thoughts that all this might be a prank, a trick of some sort, at the end of which he will find Mike antagonizing him. And then, on the other hand, there was the likelihood of what he had heard at the billiards club. What if this was a similar or perhaps the same group? He wanted to leave and run far away from his redundant professional life, that was for sure, but he was uncertain of this being the way of doing so or if this being the fruitful time of doing so. But he was also curious. Very inquisitive regarding what he was invited to. And why exactly was he chosen as a potential candidate of being a part of it? Was he being monitored all this time? If so, then how? Maybe it was a test to see whether he would succeed in it and then perhaps being promoted to a better position in the office. A plethora of contemplations swarmed across his head, while only a strand of hair stood on the top, as he crossed the three-lane diametrical road towards the nameless building.

As usual, he arrived fifteen minutes earlier than the official working hours and spotted his colleagues, all three of them from the distance, occupying their usual space besides a trashcan. Mike had decided to stick with them regardless of his promotion. But he had to subtly try and depict his superiority towards the group, which was evident when he refused to smoke the brand of cigarettes the group usually did. He held a new packet, an expensive one, not offering it to any of them. He also smoked and held the cigarette in a peculiar manner of grandiose, a manner he decided to adapt in light of the promotion, probably in the morning at the same time while our hero was also busy defeating his enemies. So he posed and twisted, wasted a few cigarettes, lamenting them internally, until finally deciding upon one, which in his opinion stood out. The pose was no less than what the cowboy usually finds himself in when he rapidly withdraws the gun during a Mexican standoff. After firing his shot, he stands still and looks on with his gun extended in parallel besides his belly button, as his opponent tumbles to the ground. Similarly, he held his cigarette between his forefinger and thumb. As he sucked on it, he would lift his chin slightly upwards, withholding the smoke until he bought his hand back down, his arm sticking out midway besides his stomach and his hand in which the cigarette was held was positioned a feet away from his belly button. While he maintained the pose, he would exhale the smoke out, left and right, as if favoring the people around him with it. Once during the act, Mike held the cigarette out but he went slightly further than the usual positioning of his hand, which led Ross to form the misconception of being offered the cigarette. So he foolishly extended his hand to receive it, almost touching it. Mike slapped his hand away in the nick of time with a look of disgust. After all, what good is a cowboy if his gun has been touched by an outlaw. Besides acquiring a pose of grandiose in relation to the art of smoking, he also attempted to change his expression. He decided to mimic the expression of a famous and good cowboy. But one might say that he failed miserably at it, that Mike for although a stylish smoker he became, had absolutely no talent at mimicking expressions. But another might say that beauty is in the eye of the beholder. Anyhow, since it could be said that the beholder of our story is Prohvark, and he is not on great terms with Mikey, hence Mikey equals to ugly. Boohoo!

Right about the moment their cigarettes burnt out, it was time to occupy their seats at the office. But not Mike, because his working hours were reduced by thirty minutes due to his newly appointed position. The three companions began to head towards the office while Mike, left alone, lit another one. When they had reached the entrance, Prohvark told them he needed to be excused, for he was in an urgency.

"What's the matter, may I ask?"

"Oh, nothing really. I just need to take a piss," said Prohvark.

"Well, there is no toilet where you are going. There are none behind the building, just inside of it."

"I know that. I have worked here longer than you have. I just have a desire to piss against the walls today."

"Haha. Like a dog marking its territory. Well, have you had those desires before too? Maybe you did.

And you have been a dog before as well. But it's only now you have showed your loyalty and trust by freely confessing them," said Rodric with a friendly sarcastic smile, "I feel our bond is becoming to grow stronger."

"Our bond? I must remind you if our bond did grow stronger, it would be that of friendship. Not the kind of bond a master has towards his slave, of a dog towards his human. For if I am a dog, you are one too, since we are equal in our standings. They say a dog is a man's best friend. I say a dog is the best and only appropriate slave for a man. For the dog enjoys his slavery. While the human does not feel like or undertake the position of inequality by being a master towards him. Anyway, the reason I decided to piss against the wall is not that I am longing for a dog or that I have become one. I just thought if celebrities and the so-called individuals we hold as role models today can piss in buckets while being under the heavy spotlight of the public eye, then why can I not do the same but only in secret."

So saying Prohvark proceeded while Ross and Rodric went inside. It was a decent thirty steps to reach the back of the building. The place was always deserted, for no one had anything to do there, but it was known behind there somewhere was a storeroom which was locked always. What might be stored inside, no one cared enough. As Prohvark walked sideways along the building, he noticed the side walls, although dusty, were spotless. No stains were to be found on them anywhere. A testament to the place not being visited at all. Oh how the side wall seemed longing to be spit upon and to be recolored by tobacco like the front wall of the building. For equality, it yearned to be like its brother, or sister, or perhaps it's better to leave out the gender of the wall in fear that it might take offense. The side wall also wished that employees leaned against it. It had a strong desire to support the soles of their shoes. To be soaked in the smokes of their cigarettes and to smell of it for the rest of their days. The glory of being an equal! The victory of it! Equivalent both in virtue and disgrace, how everything aches for it! Anyway, the reason why our protagonist had decided to walk this path was not that he wanted to mitigate himself or, as one might say in a language vulgar, to piss off. Neither was his purpose to oblige the wall in making its dream of equilibrium come true. That was just an excuse made by our clever plump figure. His main purpose had a thing to do with the secret passage mentioned in the envelope, which was hidden within the supposed storeroom that was unvisited. Even though he had not made a decision, he felt that it would all be clearer by a mere examination of the room. So it was when he did spot the ordinary-looking storeroom from a distance, which was built separately in a corner along the walls surrounding the building by three sides. He was seized by a feeling of acting upon the instructions provided to him. And the envelope all of a sudden did not seem like it was written in jest. It did not appear like a trick. It was a very serious invitation. It was true that the effect might have been aroused due to having read the envelope which he had received beforehand. For the room was so ordinary in structure, if looked upon casually, it would arouse no suspicion at all. But now having read the letter, it seemed as if the room was built with a special purpose. As if it was an integral part of the nameless building itself, and without having built that, the approval of constructing the building would be halted as well. The outer surface of the room was painted yellow while the door was maroon. With a sense of fear and awe, standing a couple of steps before it, Prohvark felt like he was at the doorstep of the mansion of an old, antiquated king. He surveyed the exterior of it like an architect with an amateurish eye, looking to redesign a project left in his care. It was instructed that the key to open the door was inside one of the bricks, the texture of which was not like just any another brick in the wall. And it would not require a man of education to determine which brick it was. The brick stood out in a fashion similar to how a bright kid stands out in the classroom amongst a group of students. Prohvark felt like a teacher whose attention is taken away from the embarrassing and shameless kids just because of the overwhelming pride he feels at having the privilege of being able to teach that one kid alone. He drove back the brick with his index finger. And truly, the texture felt like it had been spat upon by a thousand of employees a countless of times. Prohvark felt a strong inclination to put forward his nose and smell the brick to determine whether it smelled of cigarettes or not. He thought the better of it so as not to appear like a madman even though there was not a soul around who would have seen him. But who knows maybe he restrained himself to appear likeable in your eyes, Reader! Or maybe the glimmer of the key which was made visible by the push restrained him. Startled and pushed him away. The brick positioned itself back in place once he clutched the key in his hand, the way a lottery winner clutches his ticket in anticipation of the winning number being declared. Looking at the size of the key and its curves, one would confidently shout in prediction, saying, "there is no way that specific key unlocks that specific door." He would also bet his lottery number upon the prediction. Although it would be the number whose fate was yet to be declared. But neither was the holder of the key at that particular time a screamer, nor did he try his hands in lottery and confident he did feel but rarely. So he stood there for a while. Confronting the door, motionlessly. But clutching the key was he, while the door stood empty. Then a thought to exchange their fates, and in a second the key slid in the lock firmly and easily like two lovers who had embraced each other dearly after a long time. Prohvark almost turned the key, but right then, he was seized! Seized by the fear of not being on time to occupy his seat at the office. He turned around in a hurry but noticing having forgotten the two lovers in embrace, he turned back to fulfil his role as the villain, snatched the key away from its lock, and pushed the brick back to replace it where it lay surrounded again by mould and clay. The brick positioned itself on top of it while Prohvark began to walk back along the sideway towards his office on the sixth floor.

Halfway through the sideway, Prohvark abruptly halted. Facing towards the wall, he undid the zipper of his pants. What came next needs not to be jotted down in detail, for it comes every day to those who are blessed by normal conditions of the human biology. But for what reason it came? That's hard to state. Maybe he meant to fulfil the wish of the untouched wall to become like the other walls. Maybe Prohvark felt frustrated and angry at himself for not going all the way in following the instructions. So he decided to fulfil his prior convictions and to appear not as a liar in the eyes of his colleagues. Although they were made as an excuse. But how could Rodric and Ross really find out whether he had urinated or not. It's not as if they would come out, searching for wet stains on the wall and lifting their noses up to enhance the ability of their smelling sensors. Or on the other hand, would they? Gracious how far, across the ocean, does convictions lead a man!

10

With rapid steps, Prohvark rushed on towards his office like a man who is about to miss the last train departing. Entering the nameless building, he found a horde of people waiting for the elevator. At first, he stood amongst them in wait, but his patience soon ran out when a part of the crowd entered and he foresaw that maybe two parts more would enter until his turn came. So he decided he would rather take the stairs in hopes of reaching sooner. The office being on the sixth floor and considering the brevity of time, it meant that he had to ascend the stairs quickly. The task turned out to be no less than a vigorous exercise which made him regret the decision, as he was sweating like a gym instructor. A few raised eyebrows also viewed him with a similar conviction, a murmuring voice was heard saying, "Has he been jogging all the way here?" "Might have been running from rabid dogs."

When Rodric sighted him, he peeled into laughter. Ross almost did the same but sufficed himself with confusion instead. Prohvark threw himself on the seat, turning on his working device before catching his breath, waiting for it to start. Rodric had an amusing idea in his head, so he began speaking.

"Is the wall dry?" said he, Prohvark was visibly confused at the question. So Rodric elaborated, attempting to make it clear. "Seems like you have completely missed the mark," he bursted again from his repressed laughter, "And ended up pissing all over yourself."

"It's just sweat. I took the stairs in a hurry."

"Is that so? Well, Ross why don't you cement that fact and have a sniff? Ha-ha."

Ross bent his face forward and slightly lifted it upward in all seriousness, but Prohvark drew back, hurling a pen towards him that came up short and wound up on the floor. At the moment, a silence ensued but not completely because Prohvark was still panting audibly as a result of climbing the stairs. Rodric found that funny enough and chuckled again. Twice he chuckled, and every time he did, he threw his head back and corked it downwards due to which lines of excess fat revealed themselves on his neck. Those lines further led to fueling Prohvark's annoyance, without him understanding. If not for the fat, he might have let Rodric go on with his mockery, but now the lines had been crossed.

"Go ahead and pick that pen for me!" ordered Prohvark to Rodric.

"Why should I? You are the one who threw it. I already have a boss who orders me around. Don't use a similar tone as if I have asked for another one. A single boss is enough. More than!"

"Go ahead and PICK IT UP!"

"Direct your orders at Ross. It was him that made you fling the pen at him," Alas, he had no idea that Ross's neck did not reveal lines of excess fat upon chuckling.

"If you DO NOT pick the pen up, I swear to the single god needed, more than enough, that I will make sure leaving you in such a condition that you will have trouble picking up a pen ever again in your life, so as to even write with it. I will make you regret putting an effort in coming up with a unique signature for identification purposes."

"And what exactly will you do, if I don't?"

"I just told you what I would do. That I will make sure you never get to pick up pens again in your life. I will make you regret ever putting in an effort to learn and walk as a baby." "That's not what you said exactly last time!"

Both were staring at each other. An electric signal in their eyes conveyed their thoughts to each other. Prohvark was preparing for an assault. He slowly kept his hand upon the stapler at desk as if caressing it with affection, the equivalent of a warrior sharpening his sword before an attack. Rodric also sensed something was coming his way. He tightly gripped the edges of the table like a shield the three hundred Spartans utilized against the Persians. The stapler was lifted slowly with the right hand and the hand stretched beyond the back of the head. Prohvark made an attempt in deception to conceal the attack. It came in the form of using the stapler as an object to scratch a spot on the protagonist's back that was out of reach. The battlefield was quiet enough for the sound of stapler being chaffed against the back to be heard. But as the chaffing became faster, it implied that the relief from the itchy spot was almost at hand, making the attack predictable. The next moment, the stapler was bulleted towards Rodric. The foe gripped the shield tighter, and the same neck that showed lines of abundant fat now moved to the right in such a swift, smooth manner as if it was the neck of a classical Indian dancer performing after years of hard practice the attami, a movement in which the head is moved robotically from side to side. The movement certainly made Ross wonder what the outcome of the historical battle would have been if the Spartans were well specialized in the art of attami as well. The arrows and the glaives would have missed them, ending up in the forest deep or at the base of the ocean beyond the precipices of mountain. But since the war zone presently was not of such a landscape, the stapler after missing the mark ended up flush against the temple of an approaching person who unfortunately did not even know what an attami was. It was the forehead of the assistant to the Boss! No help for it...Collateral damage! The damage was painful as was evident by the assistant's jump in the air, his forehead sinking into his palms. But he did not shriek or sniffle. He maintained his dignity, his poise, with a tear at the corner of his eyes. The assistant, in resentment, front-kicked a table nearby, as if he too was a Spartan in disguise. Then he searched for another table, but luck not being on his side and only being on the side of the table at a distance, he changed his mind by slapping his forehead. He began to look around in order to clarify who had unleashed the stapler towards him. Looking in front of him, he spotted all three of them standing speechless with an expression of alarm and fear. Perhaps a word of condolence would have served them well, especially Prohvark. But they lacked those aptitudes. Only Ross stood with an open mouth, his hand on forehead as if sharing in the assistant's torment or rather of the table that was the victim of a Spartan front-kick. Nothing can be said about Ross, unless and until he nods.

"What was that?" roared the assistant. After looking around and spotting the stapler on the ground, he kicked it furiously under a table, "WHO was that?"

No answer.

"Who and WHY was that? And why me?"

No answer. Shuffling amongst the involved.

"Was it you, Ross?" I demand an answer. "Speak now. For once." But Ross just looked at Rodric, which made the assistant into questioning him, "Did that just fall out of the sky? Speak quickly or there will be trouble!"

There had been enough trouble, so Rodric began pouring all of it out. He did so intelligently, calmly, for he found himself being at no fault. The incident was explained in its entirety. Even the plight of the wall. Ross nodded once, twice, thrice. Although he sympathized with the protagonist, eyeing him with pity when the narration of the incident hit the turning points. Prohvark did not put a word in during the entire narration. Did not excuse himself. No expression of remorse. He would scratch his head and sometimes raise his eyebrows, shrug his shoulders. When the narration was over, he opened his mouth to say something. However, he was quickly overtaken by the assistant's discourse.

"When first you people joined the company, we clearly laid down the rules of conduct. Furthermore, we ourselves ironed our behaviour so we could be leaders by example. But how you guys have failed cannot be comprehended. For you have acted in a complete opposite manner to how your leaders have done and are doing currently." He tightened his tie with an air of pride before resuming. He was talking as if the attack towards him had been done deliberately with precision. "This is unacceptable, gentleman. To waste your time that belongs to the precious well-being of the company. But I am here, and as long as I will be here, the company will thrive." His tone implied a great sacrifice on his part. He further spoke in a commanding tone, "Battle. I fight till I am here. I hurt my forehead for the company. Time and again. If had the choice of going back to the start, I would reject recruiting you guys. Now it seems I have the chance once again of deciding your fate. I will have this matter taken directly to the head office for a snappy and decisive action. Let me tell you this, your chances, your odds of staying, all three of yours, are not looking great."

So saying, he walked away resolutely, not finding it worthy to wait for their reply. The assistant accused all three of them for the assault and the insult. It was too easy for him to fire or dismiss only Prohvark. He considered the insult to an extent great enough to punish all of them and to show off the magnitude of power he held over them. Prohvark dismissed the threat, as it had happened before on quite many occasions. That is, a similar kind of threat was used to enforce order and discipline amongst the employees. To drive them towards performing better. Rodric also thought of himself and of Ross to be completely out of danger. He imagined the assistant to be bluffing.

Furthermore, he thought if there was at least someone in a genuine danger, it was only Prohvark. Regardless, something was gnawing inside of him, driving him to berate the protagonist.

"Do you see what happens? Do you see? That's what happens!" Rodric shouted indignantly.

"What precisely are you talking about?"

"That's what happens when you hit the assistant on the forehead. Your colleagues and neighbours pay for it as well. Come on, man! Dude!"

"My intentions were to directly make you pay. But if it does happen indirectly, it can be said then that I did not miss my objective, but I accomplished it by thinking in an out-of-box manner. And if Ross goes with it, he goes with it! You must also hold yourself partly responsible for what has happened. If only you had picked the pen, we would be working on our keyboards right now." Here the hero himself went over, picking up the pen in a show of demonstration. Then he realized he could have done the same earlier. He realized that he let his emotions get the better of him. His emotions outwitted him, just as Rodric's got the best of him too. Prohvark felt to thinking that he was not much different from his colleagues now. That they were of the same level. Neither was he superior in morality nor was he more talented. With this thought, he began walking out of the office. Rodric yelled after him to ask where he was going, but he just waved his hand and walked away.

Prohvark took the elevator this time. Standing in front of the main entrance to the nameless building, he looked up towards the blue sky, the sun partly covered by a cloud which soon spread over it completely. He stood gazing. Not a thought stirred in his head. Now he began anticipating the cloud to cover the sun completely, and when it happened, he began to take a stroll towards the side of the building. With a resolution as strong as that of the sun to radiate through the clouds, he walked towards the storeroom. Gently going over the wall with his hand, feeling the texture of it until it seemed different at a spot. Pushing that spot, he retrieved the key to the door. Locked it in. Twisted it. He pulled down the handle of the door. Considering how long the door had remained closed, it still made no creaking sound at all. Even when he opened the door, pulling it towards him, there was not even a trace of an eerie noise. It refused to squeal. When the door opened and the dark interior was visible from the partly opened creak, at that moment, the sun also revealed itself through the clouds. Prohvark thought it was with such an exact synchronization that the sun revealed itself at the moment as if it also wanted to be present, as if it had been waiting, hanging tight, for ever so long until the door opened, so it can lend its own magnificent light on that special occasion to the darkness of the insides of the room. Now even though the sun was shining on everything, it was sparkling more brightly, more joyfully on the interiors of this room. But Prohvark yet dared not peer inside. Looking at the floor, he ventured on the premises of the little room and shut the door behind him. A complete darkness ensued. He was afraid of what the room may look like, of what it might contain, so the darkness had a calming effect on him presently and he looked around now with a sense of anticipation of looking at the same room, shortly with the lights turned on. After looking around to his heart's content, he began feeling with his hand the wall next to the door. There was the switch of the light mentioned in the instructions on the envelope. He shut his eyes before flipping on the switch. Light fell upon his closed eyelids, and he shuddered. For a few seconds, he stood still with eyes closed. Then he let his hands drop from the switch, finally opening his eyes.

11

He found himself in an ordinary-looking room, but that room was soon to reveal a great hidden secret. The room seemed to have been abandoned for a long time, and it had forgotten the presence of a human being inside of it. Only spiders and their cobwebs dangled in the corners. Even their cobwebs were empty, not having had caught any food or prey for the spider in a long time. The spiders probably from a hunger, long overdue, hoped or might have tried to subdue Prohvark under their webs. And the moment he entered the room, they prayed in gratitude for such a mighty feast-able prey. But it was all in vain, for they soon realised the extent of their power was too less in comparison to the opportunity to be seized, which was provided to them. And they only scrambled helplessly when Prohvark shut the door behind him, and their webs almost collapsed from the corners.

Prohvark wasted no time in demolishing the suspense he felt, for he quickly went to work on the instructions provided in the envelope. He had memorized the instructions and left behind the envelope. A slight feeling of anxiousness simmered on the top of his head. He thought, "Might they not ask for the envelope?" Anyway, it was too late or too daring for him to go back. Just the thought of exiting the room for the envelope and making his way back to go all over the ordeal again made him drop the idea of the envelope holding any valuable importance in allowing him to gain an entry.

So he began acting as the instructions had said. He turned around to face the door. Locked it twice by twisting the key to the left and once making an attempt towards unlocking by twisting the key to the right. He almost pulled the key out but remembered just in time that the instructions commanded for the key to be left in. Now he shut the lights off and turned it on and then shut it once again before leaving it on. And he closed his eyes both the times when the lights were shut not because the instructions said so, but only because he was afraid of the darkness. It's only when a room is dark that the mind wanders off towards imagining the things possible to fill it with. And our protagonist like most people filled the room and the darkness with horrifying images of ghosts. And goats since he had lived through being an audience for that pool game. With light, he moved on towards carrying the instructions. With haste, he attempted to carry all the steps but the step at hand slightly hesitated him. He was to pick up a dusty slipper kept on a wooden slate attached to the wall and use that slipper for beating to death a spider on the top right corner of the door. Prohvark picked the slipper up and faced the spider. He thought that this was some sort of a bravery or ruthlessness test for him to carry. He lifted the slipper and held it in air a little bit above his right ear and the dust fell off from the sole, sprinkling on the top of his curved ear and some on his shoulder. He paused for a moment of reflection. How long had the spider made his home here? Was the spider asleep? For they say dying in sleep is painless. I hope he is asleep. Certainly, it looks like it. Then he could no longer ask himself more questions or pause for any such reflections, for he felt that he was going soft and would soon give in to sparing the spider's life. Also, his hand was going numb from holding the slipper in air. So he swiftly brought the slipper down and crushed the abode of the spider. He shut his eyes from the murder, and it was good fortune he did so for upon the heavy contact of the slipper against the wall, the dust emitting spread all over his face and his eyes were saved from any particles that could possibly have entered them. With eyes shut, he thought that his cowardliness in this instance to not even be able to see the crushed body of a spider saved him from rather a misfortune. For what if the dust had gone in his eyes? He would have certainly teared up. And then 'they', whoever they were, he thought, would think of him as sentimental over the death of a spider. "All happens for good," he exclaimed loudly. Without being empathetic towards the squashed spider. He turned over the slipper for a confirmed kill. Not only was the spider dead, he was reduced to what Prohvark mistakenly thought all along was dust. And that what was all over his face, on his shoulder and on the top of his curved ear were dead spiders accumulated on the sole of that slipper throughout the years. Well, not completely. It was dead spider mixed with dust. Prohvark stared at the sole and brushed his shoulders off from the dust. And the dead ashes of spiders on his face, he let be, thinking that a soldier does not wipe blood off from his face while he is still in the middle of a battlefield, fighting, for it's bound to get bloody again. Hopefully, when the battle is done and he is done slashing through his enemies, he would wipe the blood off, perhaps even have a hot water bath. But suppose he dies in the battlefield?

Well, then who cares! Is it not better to lay dead and let one's own blood remain on the face forever than to remain alive only to wipe the blood of a stranger from one's own face for the rest of time? Strangers whom one had no reason to kill. Such was thinking our protagonist, and forgetting everything else, he wiped his face with his sleeve, as it was itching. And he wiped it good before realizing the ashes of the dead spiders were gone. Completely gone. No war signs remained. No medals of honour and valour. He sighed loudly and moved on towards carrying the final step of instructions.

The final step was to take off one of his shoes and discard it upon the table from which he had retrieved the slipper. Then he was to wear the slipper on his leg, move towards the wall facing opposite to the door of entry and begin kicking it until he had hit the right spot which would open the entrance to the underground. As he began taking his shoes off, he thought maybe he should have worn cheap toilet shoes for this occasion. But then he thought that the decision to enter the storeroom was taken in haste. Perhaps If I had planned it out, he told himself, then I would not have to leave my shoe for spiders to be crushed by any other forthcoming individual whose plight is supposedly been known.

"Wait a minute. Then it's one spider per shoe or slipper. So it was mostly dust on my face." He placed his pointy black and shiny office shoe on the wooden slate and wore the dusty old slipper and said out loud, "This is perhaps the worst shoe deal in the history of shoe deals. Ever!" Then, he thought at least the person who would arrive after him would have a possibly better deal at hand. Or at feet. So he moved on towards the wall with a shiny office shoe on one leg, and on the other, a slipper that was used by someone who had spent most of his time in and around religious shrines. He approached the wall, and the wall shivered with fear as it beheld our protagonist approaching him with the combined power of a corporate capitalist company and the power of organized religion. Anyway, the wall probably remembered the quote which goes something like, "I'm not afraid from a swarm of sharks led by a sardine, but I am afraid of a swarm of sardines led by a shark". And the quote was proved true, as Prohvark screamed in pain and clasped his leg the second time he kicked the wall by over-hitting it. The next time he stood up to find the spot again, he realized that he certainly did not have to punish the wall. Or his leg. Maybe slightly tapping or poking it until he had found the hidden spot. So he began tapping on the wall, and for the first time in his life, he thought perhaps he could have made a decent tap dancer. As he was tapping, he thought to himself, "Maybe that's it! They have already showed me what my purpose in life is. It is to become a tap dancer. I never would have known. I have to go back now and quit my job immediately. Follow a path paved by my own feet like how they used to say."

Prohvark kept on tapping; the more he tapped with no results, the more he thought it was his destiny to become a tap dancer. He tapped and tapped, as the sweat began to show visibly on his forehead, and he tapped some more as the sweat rolled down his cheek. *I certainly have to work on my weight and cardio issues if I am to become a dancer*, he thought to himself. "Perhaps I need to stop smoking as well," he said out loud. But then as he was tapping, he hit a spot and the light suddenly began to blink rapidly. He could not make his eyes blink in synchronicity with the light. So for a second, he was confused whether to see or not to see. To shut his eyes or let them be open. That was the great question. And he realized the answer was not in his hands, as he did not get to decide and the light made the decision for him by stopping to blink and remained on.

And a part of the wall carved. It carved in slowly. Then it slid smoothly to the left and revealed an elevator with a transparent glass door. An elevator that could hold only one person at a time and shaped in such a way he had never seen before. It looked like it was made by people belonging to a different world and made by a different kind of technology. Or energy. The inside of the elevator was white and with a marble that seemed to have been extracted by scraping of the sky. As Prohvark stepped forward, the glass door automatically slid upward to provide entrance. And he stepped in, first with his right foot wearing the dusty slipper and then his left. Once in the elevator, there was only space enough to turn around. So he turned around and faced the door of the storeroom through which he had entered. He contemplated his decision. Why had he come here? Should he have or have not? Where was this elevator leading him? He knew it was already too late. And the glass door of the elevator slid back downward, closing him in. Prohvark stared at the door, and in a flash, he was staring at nothing. The elevator went down so smoothly that he was unsure whether it was even moving at all. He was unsure whether it was going down or up. But he remembered the envelope and its mention being underground. Now he knew where he was going. And he was delivered.

PART 2

1

Although it didn't take much time to reach the underground, Prohvark had already fallen victim to a well and fulfilling sleep inside the elevator. Some individuals, oblivious to having reached the end of their goals, are unable to keep themselves from struggling hard. Likewise, it was way long after the elevator had stopped that he opened his eyes and was aware of reaching his destination. For a moment, he thought of going back to sleep. Not because he wanted a taste of that fulfilling rest again but just because he was afraid of what was in front of him at the underground. What exactly he had to face? What was in front of him? It was the fear of what he faced that made him hope if perhaps he fell asleep again, the elevator will take him back to the top. And this time, he would run on and out through the door of that storage room without a heartbeat of hesitation. But he shook his head out of the idea of such a sleep. For he feared there might be a hidden camera somewhere in the elevator which will record his cowardly, pretending act. So he decided to venture forth.

The handle for opening the sliding elevator door was nowhere to be seen. So he started feeling that glass with his hand. And with the first touch of his confused fingertips, the door slightly pushed back and slid up to a cold, clean breeze which kissed his face. He was caught by surprise. He enjoyed that breeze. For a second, it felt like the air-conditioned room of his office. And he thought somehow, magically, he had made it back there. But that illusion of false hope was also lifted, as he feasted his eyes upon a green, grassy open field with not a soul visible. Not a soul to be seen. There were hills which waved up and down. From afar, such silky hills that a skater with skills would have skated easily upon them. Open fields, at all fours, wherever Prohvark laid his eyes, it was the same hill going up and down. At some places, the grass had overgrown till the knee point, and they stood out like swords for they were smooth and shiny. It was a good thing that they were as flexible as a paper, or they would have caused much more damage than just paper cuts. Prohvark decided to stay away from those areas for fear of bleeding or the fear that they might contain snakes and other dangerous insects. Prohvark spun twice to confirm where he was and detect any form of civilization in the distance. But there was none. He thought that perhaps it was an illusion. He circled once again, and after a few seconds, he realized to his panic that the elevator which bought him here was nowhere to be seen. Did the ground swallow it? He asked himself. And a genuine fear seized him. He began to run, but after a quick ten feet, he realized the absurdity of running all alone on an open hill. So he put himself together again.

The cold breeze was the only comforting thing for him about this place. And the light mist which for some reason made him feel pleasant rather than invoking a fear in him. Normally, he would have thought that perhaps monsters hid away in those invisible misty distance. But now, he was thinking positively. He thought of a party going on. With music. And pizza. And a comfortable sofa. A person usually envisions relief after hardship. So perhaps that was the case here. For the journey for him, so far, was terrifying and full of surprises. So he walked a distance for a while. An hour? Half an hour? For how long he walked, he couldn't say because he did not keep track of time. He was invested way too much at what was present at hand. So he walked over to the mist. And he did so again. And again. And the mist disappeared and was visible in the distance again. And nothing else was to be seen, only hills with shiny, lush green grass, overgrown at some places. It was only after he decided to keep track of time, and when he walked then to an estimate of about ten minutes, that he began to see a couple of trees in no particular order. Trees with a girth that would require at least three men hugging it in order to cover it. Solitary trees, all made visible by an oil lamp which hanged from one of their branches. Upon spotting that light, Prohvark suddenly jumped to a miraculous revelation. Something which was obvious, but he failed to notice before. He noticed that above the grassy hills was an entire sky without a moon. So did he really travel underground? If he did, then this place must have had a roof. But there was a sky instead and without a moon. But the plains were revealed to sight and illumined by a light similar to the moonlight. This was a matter way too far for our protagonist's tiny mind to comprehend. So he just sufficed himself with a silly answer. "Maybe the light from those lamps by the branches have reached all over the place." That's what he told himself. Forgetting all about the mist and how it blocks the light from the lamp from going much further.

It's true that when we are happy, joyful, time seems to go by in a jitter. As if it were a rowboat being swept by the vigorous intensity of a tide and towards a waterfall. And when we are sad or morose, we truly feel the slow, heavy burden of time's passage upon us. As if it was a massive boulder on our shoulders, the weight of which we could fight and struggle against, up to an extent when we either can escape, wriggle away somehow or when it finally flattens us out. However, when a person is in a curious state of mind about a particular event which he presently faces, the outcome of which he is unsure of and which keeps him on the edge, at bay, knees buckling, with such an event it seems as if time completely stops at hand. Vanishes away. And it would only begin to tick again whenever the answers to the particular event were revealed. When everything was made clearer. Such was our protagonist, lost with time when he found himself in this situation, in this place. The event had replaced time. And it can happen, one can live in a such a way that he replaces the concept of time with that of events. His entire life turning into a reel of events after events. In that sense, it can be said that a specific person lived for a thousand events and another for a fifty long dragged-out events. A special one for a single event called life, the answer or the action and solution of which he struggled with until his death. And what remains to be seen is the lesson from one event and the way in which it effects the upcoming. If one was to precisely determine the first lesson he learned and work his way carefully up from there, he would have for himself a life smooth without mistakes. And if one was unable to see the mistake both genuinely or in arrogance, the mistake will keep repeating itself until he spots it or yields to it. Whether our protagonist would somehow find a way out of this event is yet to be known. But what's for sure is that the past four to five years of his work life were a single continuous, dull and soul-crushing event.

Anyway, he began a long walk towards one of those trees. Those trees marvelously stood out with the help of that burning lamp. They stood out like a lighthouse on an island. Like a lot of lighthouses on the biggest island that one could ever imagine. And he walked towards one of those trees. As he came under the light of the lamp, he decided he would take some rest and laid down against the tree. He laid down heavily, and only then realized he had a slight pain in his legs. "I must have walked for quite a long time," he said loudly. As if he was talking to the tree. Or to the lamp. Or to his leg. Or to the pain of his leg. No, he just said it out loud because he had a habit of talking to himself. But the tree certainly might have felt that he was being addressed. Who knows. If a sane, civilized, an employed independent person could talk to himself and it was considered normal by most, then a solitary tree on a grassy plain, for God knows how long just staying there all alone, could also maybe listen in hopes that he might hear a voice. It's all possible. If I can think so seriously, then the reader can, all the more, take it as a joke and laugh at it. It's all possible because as he spoke to himself, the tree shook slightly and so with it the lamp which made the light flicker and along with it Prohvark's shadow. A few leaves dropped from the branches. Prohvark was not alarmed at all because he was very tired and had lost his mental faculties of reasoning, so he thought the tree might have shaken by the impact of his leaning back. "After all, I am a bit chubby and on the fat side as well." He said to himself. But one can be as fat as two sumo wrestlers and he will still fail to shake a leaf out of that tree with all his might. Anyhow, he quickly fell asleep as a couple of leaves fell on his lap and the lamp slowly swung back into place.

2

Prohvark woke up. This time without a pretending desire of going back to sleep. He awoke rejuvenated, with a sense of taking on this world which he faced. After all, it was a decision which he made himself. So he stood up and the leaves fell from his lap, down upon the grass. Probably, the only two leaves which were on the ground due to the only activity which happened in the entire place. And the wind from the movement of Prohvark quickly springing to his feet shook the lamp a little. But with a slight touch of his finger, he stopped the lamp at its place. And he looked at the smooth, silky streak of fire. A fire so smooth that if it was a shade smoother, it would reveal the person's face, acting as mirror. Prohvark took a few steps back and rubbed the itch on his back against the tree and got in the mood to prepare himself for the journey. For the walk. For the stroll, whatever was in store for him. The last time in store was a spider, a dusty slipper and a secret passage. So he thought to himself, things become better as time passes on. Perhaps this time, the spider might have trapped a delicious, barbequed steak for him to feast upon in its web. And maybe a shoe shiner was out there on the field who would make for him his dusty slipper brand new again. Or would give him another one to wear. For sure, the shoe shiner would give him company and some viable information. Hopefully, the secret passage would also transform itself into something else. Like maybe his bed. And he would wake back up in that good old, dirty apartment again. With such a positive attitude, which only the citizens of a country under the rule of a just and delightful king possess, he moved on. As he laid his eyes upon the panorama of the majestic field in front him, the barbequed steak crossed his mind again. And he realized that like the one who failed to take his passport with him while on his way to the airport, Prohvark too failed to take with him a tiffin while embarking on this picnic of an adventure. And he almost pulled his hair out when he realized he had not a drop of water on him as well. It felt like a colossal failure. He felt amateurish. "LUNCH BOX! A CAKE! ANYTHING! A PIECE OF BISCUIT! A BOTTLE OF WATER!" he roared at the plains. Such hopeless roars one could only scream when he was completely alone. And if loneliness could have been present physically, he would certainly have felt the impact of that screaming voice, a despair in them much powerful and defeating than what's in the nature of loneliness itself. At such a defeat, loneliness would have perhaps broken down in tears himself, feeling like an old grandmother who has just being kicked out of home by her very own relative. But since both loneliness and the roars lived together for now in the same house, in this case an open and spacious house, the body of our protagonist, loneliness need not fear of being that poor victim of a grandmother. Now it was a grandmother which lovingly fed our hero, that is perhaps why he had on oversized tummy. And the mist in the distance felt the roar of his voice too, as they were misplaced an inch from their usual position. "Why didn't I forget to bring my stomach as well! I'm like that spider in the storage room. Maybe worse. Way better, grateful, the spider might be in comparison to me because I thought of barbecues. BARBECUES! And what I deserve now are insects actually. And that is probably what I will have to eat if I must!" The grateful spider, if he had heard such a praise in person, he would have cried his eyes out. Eyes, all eight of them. Four time more the tears, compared to human beings. Perhaps, after taking compliments, the spider shows more gratitude as well. But alas, there was no spider or his webs upon this grassy plain. And only the visible tears of our protagonist who squatted down, with his face in hands, against the tree again. His back was itching, but he did not rub it against the tree this time in a stupid attempt to torment himself for his mistake. Or perhaps, there could have been a spider lurking in there, which he was refusing to squash in the rub in a show of generosity and an acceptance in humility, considering the greatness of that spider who was so well-behaved when it came to his appetite. So he just squatted motionless, without hope, feeling now like the citizen of a country at war, a recession, facing food shortages and an embargo with the king nowhere to be seen.

He looked up at the light of that lamp, and a hope unleashed itself in him. "There must be others out here!" How else were the lamp lit before he even got here. He rubbed his face with his hands and got up again, willing to move on. He picked a random spot at a distance, another tree to walk towards. And he began walking again. At times looking for signs of any existence. Maybe a path was carved in the grassy plains due to a caravan walking through it. He thought. Maybe someone threw a piece of plastic wrapper on the grass. There was no way people would be so considerate about preserving the beauty of this place which made him doubtful again. "Perhaps because no human had been here that it is so clean, without a blemish, like a part of the Amazon. The jungle. Or perhaps like the head of the one who owns Amazon." But he didn't know that Amazon is spoiled right now as well. So the place was like a piece of Mars. The planet. Oh, wait. Humans have made their abode over there as well. He began to look for other signs. Any signs. But there was none at all. He was doubtful whether he himself was walking there and wished for a mirror somewhere nearby. Was it a day since he was on the plain? Half a day? He began to calculate and couldn't come to a proper conclusion. With such thoughts, he reached the random place which he had chosen to walk towards. And finding the same old emptiness, he chose another spot below a tree.

Something different happened as he was walking towards the new random spot. He tripped down and fell because he was exhausted. That is what happened. He laid there on his back, looking at that moonless sky. He thought maybe he was the moon because he had just fallen down. Then he saw there was not a single star on that sky as well. With tears in his eyes, he hoped again and thought maybe others have fallen down here as well. And sleep was beginning to get heavy upon his eyelids. They were slowly giving in and closing down. They were shut. And sleep almost took him away for dreams, but a drop of rain fell on his cheek. At the thought of a raindrop, he immediately sat up. Looking at the sky, a couple more of them fell on his cheek. He waited no more to open his mouth wide, so he could catch each drop and make an attempt to not waste any. The rain began to drop fiercely. As if its only mission was to suffice the thirst of our protagonist. But the thirst was quenched, and the drops were wasted in thousands. Prohvark wished he had a bottle to save some for use further down the journey. But since he had not a bottle, he decided to put the rain to other use, so he began to dance wildly in the falling rain. He truly danced to the best of his ability because there was literally no one watching. He began to enjoy it. Circling around. Arms waving. Jumping. The rain kept falling harder, maybe it enjoyed the dance as well. But since it had no voice, there is no way we can tell. And our protagonist was very busy dancing too, so he had forgotten all about talking loudly or talking to himself. Perhaps he could have sung a song, but he never had the skills, and furthermore, it would have taken away from the music of the rain falling down upon his skin. He danced for a while, until he felt that he would exhaust himself too much and would feel the pangs of hunger sooner. So he sat down and just took it all in. He opened his mouth again after he had stopped breathing hard from that tiring dance and drank some more of that rainwater. Then he ran to the nearest tree under which he could take a shelter, for the rain began to fall with such a ferocity that it was becoming harsh upon his skin. As he rushed towards the nearby tree, he clumsily hit his head against the lamp hanging from the branch. And the lamp crashed to the ground. Then he slipped and went headfirst into the tree, which left him with a combination of dull pain but also a burning one because he had chaffed his head against the grainy texture of tree trunk. The massive tree trunk carved in an outlandish weird manner upon the impact. It revealed a similar kind of elevator through which he had just come to this grassy plain. But the inside of this elevator, the walls of it, seemed like it was made of a material incurred by the scrapping of the moonless night sky. Prohvark immediately jumped in, as for him it was an opportunity he feared he would miss. Inside the elevator, he turned around to have one last look at the grassy plains he was going to leave behind. And he saw the rain had stopped and it was as if it never poured in the first place. And he had a feeling it was the last time he would see this place or ever be in the presence of a place like this. And truly it was. As the fire from the lamp which fell down began to show obvious signs of spreading till whatever extent this paradise reached. It was spreading as quickly as a matchstick burns and was already turning parts of the beautiful green grass into something which resembled the tufts from the wool of a black sheep. It would go all the way ahead in front and circle its way back to the tree in the pit of which was the elevator in which our protagonist was currently perspiring. The elevator door slid in tight and no smoke from the fire spreading made its way through. But the smoke hid from sight that marvelous plain, perhaps the plain did not want a last, farewell memory of it burning to ashes for our protagonist to take away. And so it was. So it was. Prohvark thought to himself that he would never dance again, not even on the day of his own wedding, not even on the day when Mike gets demoted, the way he did on the night of this moonless sky.

3

The elevator arrived at the destination. But our protagonist was far from it. And it's the story of him which matters to us. Unlike the last time, he was not able to fall asleep. His mind held him awake in a curiosity of what was to come. The first spectacle of the underground, the first instance, shook him like never before. So what another floor might bring was hard for him to imagine. Perhaps, it would bring a desert in which it rarely rains. And how would a fire ever burn sand. What could possibly be his escape?

The door opened, and he stepped out, shirt soaking from the rain in which he danced above. The sun shone directly into his eyes. So he had to keep them close. But the rays of the sun were just upon his body. Comforting. The rays of it also served well towards the drying of his suit, which was beginning to get annoying with the way it stuck to his body. And it was unfortunate that he wore a white shirt made of a very thin material on this day. For it also revealed the excess lines of fat on his tummy. And only his right nipple, for the shirt was about dry enough on the left side. There is naked. There is partially naked. And there is much more partially naked. The fact that only one of his nipples was exposed made him much more embarrassed, made him feel like the third way. Why was he embarrassed? Perhaps, he again thought there was a camera somewhere. Even though there wasn't. It felt that way because at the office there were cameras on all corners and at every hallway. So he had lived under a sense of surveillance for quite a while. And that sense often carries on always. Without there being devices of control or without eyes looking for any. Or even thinking about it. The sense remains always. That sense is what establishes order in people. And embarrassment.

The sun was no longer as cruel on eyes, but his beating heart from fear was. So he still waited an instance before lifting away his hand with which he shielded his eyes from the sun. Eyes open, in front of him lay the familiar premises of his high school. A place in which he had spent some good memories. Perhaps the only good memories which he could still recall if he ever wanted. A treasure of memories, hidden and buried by its owner somewhere far and remote. Treasure, which never again the owner worried about digging out. Hence, which was of no use to him. The kind of treasure which a stranger will not bother as well to dig out. Memories forever lost. Never to be found. Even after the body decays under the ground and the emptiness of the skeleton is revealed. Such a skeleton is only of use and benefit to the archaeologist. And our protagonist did not have a classmate or a friend who frequented the same school in front of him with a bright idea of undertaking such a profession. Now here he was, faced with a campus from the past, forced upon him was some digging. Perhaps a shovel would have done him good. But a person who forgets food for picnic will often forget a shovel at the graveyard.

Prohvark stood for a while and let slid his eyes upon that

familiar structure. A structure which had ingrained itself on the map of his mind. He stood there with such an amazement, such a feeling, he felt as if something which only belonged to his mind, which had its root and foundation built in the insides of his brain was now and now only constructed on the physical realm outside. It was as if a part of his imagination was visually presented before him. And he began to take slow steps forward, began to take steps on his imagination. The feeling of nostalgia hit him hard. But thanks to his stature and tummy, he was able to take the impact, still standing and moved forward. There was a feeling in the air, the atmosphere, which made him sure that it was the final day of his high school. And it was right after the final exams were over. He looked at the distance, and what did he see? His best friend, the same old, unchanged, in age and appearance and that careless expression, together with which he had buried those treasure of a memories.

This part of the campus used to remain mostly vacant. Not completely vacant, but in comparison to the size of the part and the people present, it was like a bit of sand crumbs in the shoe. There are certain spots, whether it's in the park or in the restaurant or somewhere at the campus of a school: a spot not frequented by any soul at all, staying empty, could hold the best of memories, if one happens to spend some time in it. The activity, no matter of how low a consequence, perhaps will stay the most memorable one. And it could be a lacklustre activity performed on a daily basis, but performing one time that same activity in that specific unfrequented spot, it becomes as if the activity imprints itself physically on the heart and leaves footprints engraved upon one of the veins. Like smoking, a daily activity, but having that one smoke with a friend somewhere in the corner, under a tree amongst a bunch of lined-up trees upon which was neither a sign of a bird or a nest, that smoke becomes something special. Maybe in a way the spot thanks us forever in gratitude of providing it with company. In this case, a curse from the tree and a wish for the smoker to quickly go away from under its shade and stop choking it. For so many years, not a soul under its shade and not one upon its branches. And now came two with cigarettes. As good as coming with an axe to chop it down. Furthermore, such a spot could also create an effect of a long-lasting love for that activity performed under it. In this case, for an unobservant eye, it could lead to a stronger addiction of nicotine when in fact it was a bond with the atmosphere itself. But let's say if a game of marbles, famously known as Kanche in South Asian countries, was to be played under it, the boys who played, their love for the game will increase twofold. Perhaps then they would not enjoy playing the game on a crowded street as much as they would somewhere under trees upon that slightly wet sand.

Some other students were present as well at the spot, busy in their petty talks, whatever it is that students talk about, which seems so important for them. And which at that time in the past was important to our protagonist as well. The students with their bags and a unique style of their own, a style which would sadly be lost as they would grow up and face the seizing, devouring premise of the real world outside. When he was a student himself, it always felt like everyone was staring at him and at each other. But now, they seemed very focused and fixated upon those petty conversations which occupied them. Prohvark couldn't believe his eyes at all that was happening. And when such an unreal thing happens to fall upon a person, that person will always rub his eyes, thinking that he might be dreaming. But our protagonist was not like any ordinary person. Boy, was he something special. He was a professional employee on the premises of a high school campus. And he thought that perhaps all of this was a movie and began a search in his pockets for the remote to change this mystery channel. And since no remote was found, his second thought was sleep, only that he was dreaming could now explain all of this. He began to rub his eyes with his shirt's sleeve, which were dry by now, wishing for it to be wet, so it could wake him up better and quickly. But even if it was wet with the call of the morning prayer, it would still not wake him up. First because he was one who had prayed not for a long time and had stopped caring. And second, because he was not sleeping at all. All this was happening.

He observed his friend from a distance. And his friend with bowed head, sat on cream-colored marble steps, observing the grass, small black ants crawling around. The friend was attempting to observe, to keep in sight, at the same time as many ants possible. Sometimes it would be four at a time, and then one would disappear and another appear. Under his watchful eye, he had decided to keep eight ants collectively because that was the number of subjects to succeed in for graduation. The max he had managed altogether was six. The number would drop to four and five and a sense of despair and fear would make him frown. His stare shuffling in a hypnosis of failure. He would feel a personal grudge, a direct enmity with the ant which escaped. As if the ant was the culprit who during the test refused to show to give him answers of the questions from the paper which he did not know. A stubborn unlikable ant of a classmate. The teacher's pet. The teacher's ant, but presently the best friend felt like the monitor. While busy under the spell of this activity, Prohvark observed him for a while until the feeling of recalling old love for his old friend flattened out and was replaced with a sense of anxiety, which made him want to squeeze out through another way and avoid interacting all together. He was afraid of his best friend. Afraid of what he would say and what our protagonist would reply. He wasn't this afraid even of his teachers and their questions while being a student. A nervousness more intense and unlike the time when he initiated a conversation once with his crush, the memory of which also resurfaced along with this event. Anyway, he looked for a way out, he turned around to his dismay, once again the elevator which bought him here was nowhere to be seen. In vain, he imagined a helicopter or a private jet nearby. Which if without a pilot, he would have drove himself even though he couldn't ride a donkey. First, because the donkey might have trouble carrying his weight, like how once said the teasing boys. Secondly, just because he had never ridden one. And would want to train his palm for a good old slap on the butt, which he had not the experience of. Anyway, as he was shifting around for ways out, he heard that familiar voice calling out to him. Calling out his name. And once again, hearing the sound of that voice melted all that was disturbing him. Just the sound of his friend's voice felt like the saddest melody of homesickness, of nostalgia in the entire world. That voice, as well as the sound of the loud morning alarm, which makes one cry and wish he could go back to sleep again. Those sounds are truly equal. And he used a similar strength which stops a person from going back to sleep help him with holding on to those tears. And with that strength, Prohvark looked at the direction of his friend and saw his waving hands urging Prohvark towards him.

Our protagonist walked that slow walk. It was the same lazy walk which he had as a student. And which changed with lifestyle. Perhaps with the weight he had gained. His friend called out his name again, and for an instance that melancholic feeling seized him, but he got the best of it. For a second, he looked at his friend and then took the rest of the walk with head bowed down, until he was close enough, halting in front of the sneakers his friend was wearing. That old familiar unlaced, white sneakers with three strips of black running in between them. A bit dirty with sand. A wiggly line of blue ink on the top corner of the right one. At this point, even the sight of those shoes almost bought our protagonist to tears. And knowing the relationship of best friends, his friend might have said," Yes, you might proceed, slave, in kissing them." So he quickly looked away and tried again to muster gazing at his friend right in the eye, but he mistakenly looked over the head and the curly black hair of his friend. Prohvark had forgotten that his friend was rather of a short stature. And the colour of his skin seemed not quite as dark to his eyes now. It was a soft light brown.

"What you lookin' at over there? Some chick, huh!" His friend himself looked behind to see what it was. Prohvark made no reply. And as his friend was looking away and behind. Looking over the bushes, for he preferred a girl of height,

Prohvark observed his friend, took in once again all that familiar aspects which could perhaps overwhelm him and make him cry unexpectedly. But no matter how many times one visits the beach and watches the waves crashing upon the shore, one can still let it make one cry. And sometimes they do, without one having to try. Anyway, the best friend preferred girls with height, and Prohvark always thought that revealed a formidable quality of his best friend. For many people out there would feel insecure standing next to a girl who is taller than them. Most people as in the students of that age, in their stupid insecurities felt that way. While his best friend, so courageous, had even made quite a few attempts at scoring with girls, girls so tall in comparison to him that if he was to stand on their shoulders, the entire length would still not amount to that of a giant. Or so the other boys used to tease and say. And in his attempts, the best friend would mostly return empty-handed. And to the voice of silly feedbacks, which never deterred him from trying again. Sometimes our protagonist would be proud to have been blessed with such a cherry out of the tree. Prohvark had once said to his friend, "If courage was the only thing required at winning girls, by now you would have had a girl the size of a streetlight pole. But there are other things required as well. Like skills and a certain talent, which can be of help in climbing those poles with ease." Prohvark recalled how his friend had laughed at this comment, and a smile spread across his cheeks.

His best friend looked back at him and noticed that smile.

"You feeling really lucky about those papers, huh. Well, me too, you know. I was playing a game right now sitting there. A game which for sure predicts our passing the papers or not, and I won according to the rules. Which means I will pass them for sure. That will show them all. Those teachers they doubt us. They really do. So full of themselves. Can't wait to not see their faces again."

Prohvark just smiled his old smile, gently patting his friend on the back. His friend went on to explain the game he was playing. He precisely, with a seriousness in his tone of both that of a mentor and a proud inventor of the game, explained to Prohvark the rules and the requirements for a victory. Then they both sat down, inches close, shoulder to shoulder upon that marble as one.

"Go ahead. Try to lock on to eight of them at the same time. I did at the first attempt. No shit, man. No shit! I'm not boasting really. You see. Because I know I invented this game. So it's easier for me to win it as well. Those pesky ants. Huh!"

Prohvark sat through this memory again, knowing well how it was to unfold. But he enjoyed it still, perhaps better than he did the first time. Like watching your favorite movie again. Or like going fishing. He had already gone to fish, and now he was back home to make a barbeque out of it. At this moment, when the incident happened in the past, he had lied in order to be on equal terms with his friend who had lied as well. Prohvark lied and said he had been successful at encompassing them all, after which both of them just moved on with their day. But in the present, knowing well how the event was to unfold and knowing his friend in his attempt had failed to encompass eight ants as well, he just said without hesitation that he was unable to achieve the task. He stuck with the truth after genuinely trying to create an invisible circle in which he could entrap the ants.

"You know what, pro. I have already won at this game. But If I try again, who knows, one pesky ant might keep squeezing out. Luck is a bad thing ya know. So why not change the rules of the game. You know. Mainly for you. I can still win this one if I want to. But I suppose, an easy rule. Which we can win together. Much fun. Yeah, let's do this. Four me. Four you. Let's get them pesky ants! Time to get to work, Prohvark!"

His best friend quickly got done with telling him the new rule. It was a very simple one, not needing to be explained. For it happens. Like how bodies tired and sleeping from a hard day's work are not in time able to wake up to the jolt of the earthquake and the sounds of the crumbling roofs. So were the unfortunate, unmoving group of ants in a corner too, which the friends chose away from the grass for their easy visibility, unable in time to hear the tittering laughter of those friends and the crashing sound from the sole of their sneakers against the canvas in between which they were crushed to sleep forever. Two friends and their tittering laughter on an empty side of the campus where nothing else was going on. A few other students discussing the farewell party and a depiction of the ants' farewell to the world. All the same. After the friends accomplished their act of both killing and burying the ants to smithereens at the same time, they walked away completely sure of the outcome of the papers too. And it was not that they only crushed those pesky ants, but they also did with those stamping feet the grim, negative expectations of the teachers towards them. It also cannot be said that those ants died for nothing. For it was true, both of them passed every paper. And in a way, the ants died predicting themselves a victory of the future. That their death was in truth.

Whether they knew it or not. However, stamping on oblivious ants by no means is a sealing, a solution beforehand, for any mystery which you might be facing in a time upcoming ahead. Unless, you are a baby, around two to three years old, who is looking for a way to find an answer to the boredom he is facing at hand. In that case, it is an activity which for sure provides with some deadly entertainment.

4

Like how the giant named war, with his massive feet and strides, walks and hovers over a country and its people, but when the statistics are at front, there is only a mention of casualties faced by the army and the soldiers in the forefront. Not immediately the innocent with limbs and families lost. So did our protagonist and his friend too walk away from the scene. The ants forgotten. Nonexistent. Almost like it was not an act of deliberation, which just happened so casually as they were walking down to get some groceries and oblivious to a few ants under their feet on the ground. For a matter which is of such a miniscule importance, does it really matter if done deliberately or unknowingly?

So the friends walked. Tired from the day. They had to walk from a part of the hallway of the school to exit and make their way towards, "the cave", as they used to call it, their hangout place.

The hallways were empty, and the reason for it was there being a short fifteen-minute farewell speech by one of the teachers at the assembly hall where all the students were currently present and wishing for that dull speech to end soon. Just once a student hurried past them in the opposite direction. Probably looking for his bag or a pen which he had forgotten upon the table or under the desk. Looking at the speeding student flying past them, Prohvark's best friend was also suddenly reminded of his pen and a book upon which he made rough sketches. So they decided they would retrieve those as well. And it so happened that the classroom fell along that hallway, perhaps if it did not, they would have decided it was a book and a pen which was of no consequence anymore. Like a shoe which is taken with the tides of a river and the barefoot guy watched it being swept away, already thinking of a new pair to buy. Telling himself, they were worn out anyway, as he throws the other shoe for the river to devour as well and continues barefoot to the destination he was headed.

They halted before the door of that classroom and the best friend kicked it open with a forceful leg, thinking in his wisdom that the class would be empty, all the teachers and the students having gone to the assembly. But he was gravely mistaken. As there sat on the chair, the classroom teacher with a vicious, angry look in his eyes, which made both Prohvark and his friend buckle to a halting stop. Once again, Prohvark was the victim of his friend's daringness. It usually happens in a friendship of two very close friends that the one will always have a share in equal as well with any act of the former. Whether it's an act of insolence such of now or whether it's an act worthy of an applause. That act is a major part, it's half the personality of that very friend. An act which the latter would not pursue or even think of doing, but the consequences of which he will bear as well. The same thing which also holds them together. Which completes that friendship. For both, the friends get to experience the fruit, bitter or sweet it does not matter, but nevertheless a fruit of a different universe. A fruit of a different tree, bearing strange fruits, allowed for them to enjoy. That's what holds the friendship. That. And knowing the roots of their unique trees have begun to grow in each other. In the case of this friendship, Prohvark was the one inside whom the roots usually made their way to unwanted places. A pain in the ass. He often had to bear the punishment of the daring and outlandish things his best friend would do and in which he was forced to tag along.

Anyhow, the friends were buckled by that vicious look, the look which was not as powerful when faced with a class full of students. A full class with the force of a collective power always overpowered that angry vicious look, transforming it into a plea of disappointment. But that look had caught them now and deservedly. The class teacher pursed his lips and the already thick moustache stood out more vividly as it covered the entirety of his lips, like a turtle shell. A moustache that was already the butt of a collective joke to the classroom. And without the help of those lips which were quite thick themselves but pursed in now, without the lips deviating a bit of limelight away from it, the moustache had the power of not only a butt but an entire hut of a collective joke. A hut empty, wanting to be filled with humor and silly jokes with a sign, a board upon which was written 'moustache'. And only finding themselves at the threshold of such a hut, both the friends roared into a laughter, a laughter loud and intensified due to the class being empty. A roar of laughter, which even buckled the hut and shook its door, for the class teacher in a feeling hard to decipher began to unpurse his lips. The lips slightly parted now and even worse because the moustache had begun to bend and creep into the mouth, hanging loosely and hiding from sight partially his tongue. And laughter overwhelmed the friends as if it wanted to escape out of their belly and take a look in person at that thick, hanging moustache, almost on the verge of entering into another, wet world.

"Alright. Okay. That's enough," smiled the teacher with a shake of his head. It was not a shake of disappointment or a shake which said he felt disrespected. But rather a shake which implied, "Same old, same old students." With probably a tinge of 'never change' somewhere in there converting to a smile.

"Alright. Alright." He said again in a defeated voice, as the friends were showing no signs of stopping, whereupon he began to play with the pen and the book kept upon his table. Something which the friends had come for. Now in the hands of teacher and finally at sight converted the laughter into a tittle, made it die out and then completely.

"Okay. Looks like the both of you are done. Alright. That was a good laugh you had there. Last day of school, boys. Done and over with. Truly, there is no other day like this. Hopefully, looking back upon it and all the good times, hopefully, it will be easier upon your tears in comparison. What a classroom. What a batch! Many have come like you, and many will go. Many. Many. I myself will teach in another school. I have been contemplating the decision for a while. But the answer is becoming transparent. I think I might depart as well. My last year in this school. With you guys. Truly, it was the best, my favorite batch. Truly."

And saying this, he looked forward to once upon gaze on that empty class which he taught and perhaps imagined it full. He slid his eyes upon those empty chairs. Empty desks. Thirty of them. In a way, one can say the classroom exists independently of ideas concerning it. A much bleaker place in comparison to even the graveyard. For if one does enter the graveyard, he can say with a surety that a specific piece of land, the grave, belongs to a person forever, and none can take it away from him. The classroom belongs to no one at all. It is an entity, a universe and all the desks, the chairs contained within are like a sea belonging to that universe, a sea of hopes, dreams and half-assed ambitions in which year after year students test themselves. And some drown in it, some learn how to swim, while some with an empty bucket or bottle fill how much ever of that water possible and take it away with themselves. The person who swam might find to his heartbreak, in a future sometime, that swimming is an activity he no longer enjoys. Similarly, it can be said the person who dropped out in actuality wasn't a failure, but provided with an easy lifeline a rowboat which fell from the sky. While a teacher could possibly throw a lifeline, a water donut towards the direction of his favorite student. There it was the classroom, empty for a while, waiting for the next batch of daydreaming students. And the desks like seas. Thirty of them. Thirty times the length of the entire sea on earth. Thirty students, thirty trees, the fruits of which were partially tasted amongst each other. The bitter one always getting the class teacher. The class teacher in his gaze paused a while at Prohvark's, and besides it, the desk of his best friend. He pursed his lips again and slightly shook his head. Then he let his palms go over his face and all the way through his hair and to the back of it. And he checked slightly his hair and put them in place where they were not. The friends did not laugh this time at those pursed lips. They just stood there. Knowing not how to feel. What to say. All they wanted was to get that book and pen, for which they regretted coming now, and to get out of the empty classroom, the emptiness of which they felt unbearable even when it was stuffed with the bickering of all the students present.

"You came for those. Here. You have made good rough sketches." The teacher slid the book upon which was kept the pen to the edge of the table on the side of which the friends were standing. Prohvark picked them up for his friend before murmuring,

"Yes, Sir."

Yes sir. And that was all. An epitome. The relationship never making it any further than that. It's like an 'I love you' but serving exactly to the extreme of the opposite way. That is, unless a student falls in love with the teacher. Then it becomes a mixture frowned upon by society. The friends turned around to leave and they also paused their gaze for a while on those empty chairs; all they saw was an empty chair. An empty electric chair. Their sentence was pardoned and it was over. And as they exited that classroom which felt like a jail, they closed shut the door as softly as possible in order not to disturb or reveal the state of being a prisoner to the teacher who sat now sullenly, all alone. It was true that year after year, the teacher would consider retiring and tell himself the best batch he had just been through. But evolution works in each and every way. And he stayed, along with the rigid moustache, a couple years more. And the hut of humor by then, probably, was about the size of the nameless building in which Prohvark was employed.

5

So the best friends walked on towards the high school's gate for an exit on their way towards the group of friends who were loitering around for their return. The exhaustion from the laugh was the only thing stopping them from succumbing to fits of laughter again. But the memory of the empty classroom and the teacher alone did become a cracking tale to tell. A tale which upon recollection would make them laugh in a zeal of about half than when it actually did on the first instance of occurring.

They walked towards the exit and the towering voice from the farewell speech, although muffled by the walls of corridor, could be heard quite audibly. Walking inside the corridor, the sound from the mic did seem like someone was speaking with a towel stuffed in his face and mouth. But if focused upon, the words would become decipherable. And since the voice on the mic was that of a familiar teacher, the speech pattern and style of which the friends were often tortured to, it became for them much easier to understand. And as his muffled voice filled the corridor, they also imagined his puffy face and that shirt tightly tucked in like Humpty Dumpty, making his tummy appear much roundly firmer than it was. And certain words, the way they flew out of the mouth, also made them sure that his pointy finger was shaking at the sky.

"My pupils. Today you will be leaving this honorable and

beloved school. And your respected teachers. But the time you spend here will be unforgettable to you. And painfully to us. Oh, you screaming children. Very naughty. You have to carry the values this school taught you. And do not become a stain upon the school's reputation. And do not let your teachers down. We are like your second parents. Or better. We worked so hard to teach you lessons. Do not let our hard work go to waste. Also keep up in sports. Be athletic. And while going to get groceries, be kind. In the restaurant before eating the food..."

The friends were almost at the door of exit and the speech from the mic was becoming unclear. The teacher on stage was one of those teachers who don't really fit the requirements of their profession completely, who are unable to be efficient in their work but are hired because the quality in which they are lacking is covered by an attribute of some other sort. Teachers who are annoying when they speak on their own subject of specialty but become unbearable when they began to show you a glimpse of that attribute without which they would have been possibly fired. The teacher on stage taught the friends physical education. Without having any physique of his own. But one might say to not judge a book by its cover. In that case, even the contents inside the book were like one line a page. He neither seemed like one, neither spoke like a knowledgeable one. But he had still managed to keep the job because of the other attribute. He would sometimes partly become a motivator. Or would use lines from religious scripture, of which he did not have complete knowledge as well. And in those instances, the normally annoying tone would transform into a tone which made him appear further despicable. "Oh, here we go again." They would tell themselves as they would lay back completely on their chairs to embrace the impact of the oncoming tirade. By the time the friends reached the exit door, the physical education teacher was almost on the verge of transforming into that spiritual Guru. And since it was the last farewell speech, he would also try to maintain that Zen-like state for as much as he could. Until he became tired himself. Until the children who were not rebelliously brave enough to squeeze out of the line were reminded of the Albert Einstein's quote: time is relative. Perhaps, they wished for the man on stage to change forms back to being a physical education teacher and to stretch out on the stage in funny postures. The friends felt sorry for all those present at the assembly hall.

And with that last memory of the school's premise, a teacher alone thinking about his future and a teacher on stage attempting to direct the children's future and with a one last funny tale in the pocket, the friends walked on towards 'the cave'. A cave in which waited for them five more friends of similar character. In a spot surrounded by the friendly atmosphere, they were like sleeping bats, and they only began to be five rebellious black bats, screeching on the faces of the dominating teacher while in the classroom. The two best bats went on slowly towards their hangout place. The best friend was smoking and our hero beside him, walking confidently. Now, they were out of the school's premise, and behind them they heard that familiar music playing on loudspeakers from the assembly hall. A music, a note on the piano which was played when there was a change in programme. A music which currently signified the finality of a motivating speech, but which also put our protagonist in a trance-like state.

There are pieces of music, which one hears somewhere occasionally in childhood or like the Bedouin who hears the wind slithering over the sand. And as time passes, hurdles arise which stop the music from reaching the ears of the listener. Whether the music went out of taste. Or the person playing it died. Or whether the one hearing the music moved to make his abode some other place. But often times, the Bedouin if he hears the wind flowing through the leaves, it might also remind him of the smell of that lovely desert, and a longing will arise within him to cut down all those trees in an attempt to lay the land a barren world of sand. So too the music playing to signify a change in programmes, which our protagonist heard a thousand times at school, made him forget that he was grown, made him forget the underground and the nameless building. Made him forget all that was dead, and he was simply dead present walking once again besides his friend like they had never departed. He had never made excuses. No plans were postponed. Furthermore, those pieces of music might make one long for a last time. The listener might realize the music he heard in childhood meant many things, like for one it meant an end of session. While some others just hated the sound of it on their ears. But if all of them were to listen to the same piece of music years later, in a future when all were grown up, the music only means one thing—time and tide waits for no man. And man plays his own music to the ticking drums of the clock. They either ride or sail or swim through the tide, the tide which is unaware of the inconsequential presence of their tiny bodies mired with them.

The hangout place was a bench upon a structure of artificial sea. A structure which looked a lollipop from a vertical, bird's eye view. A lollipop, the sweet candy ball of which was over a puddle of rainwater. And the spot, the bench which they sat upon, was right on the tip of that sweet circle looking over the sea. So the friends walked on the plastic cylinder holding that sweet ball, a straight solid concrete pathway towards the circle's tip. Bricked by red and grey, in between which were wooden benches in parallel to the straight line. And between every bench was a tree. The pathway, on both sides was bogged up with large minerals rocks, against which the sea water did not crash but seeped and sailed slowly in between since it was an artificial flow. The entire feeling coupled with the sounds of the waves and chirping birds on those trees completely immersed our protagonist, making him forget the illusion of the underground, perhaps like watching an 8D, 9D, or even a 13D movie.

Prohvark saw the friends at a distance. And he remembered this day like it was yesterday. One of the friends sat straight on the wooden bench, the other besides him took the lotus position, while the third was standing, leaning over the rails, watching the view of that artificial sea. A view which he complained about for not having the ability to stir within him the boiling surge of feelings like how a real sea usually does. The circle had established a friendship that understood and related in a brotherly way, even when the faces were looking away from each other. Like magnets. Or like the clock and how it is filled with numbers on all the fours, which further makes it easier for the eye to make out the time by a look at the hour hand. Our hero and his best friend were at a distance of about ten feet when the standing one turned around to spot them.

"What took you guys so long, man? Running after girls. Ohhh, don't tell me you guys actually attended the assembly. We all agreed we were gonna squeeze out on it, man." Said the standest.

"No. No. We did not."

And the best friend went on to explain the tale of that poor hanging moustache who almost drowned in a filthy gutter, the teacher's mouth. At which the friends laughed like they too were present and watching from the window perhaps. Prohvark also had a blissful laugh at the sight of the old silly heads laughing in a chorus, a unison, an impossible one like bonding together the symphonies of Mozart and Beethoven. Although great on their own, they would make deaf anyone who tries an attempt of listening to it together a thousand times in order to enjoy. In a foolish attempt to take in the greatness of both. Or to prove that you could be a fan of both. But the unison of the friends laughing became bearable amongst them because it was listened to by the single ear of young and friendly compassion. If not listened by a single ear, then it would have adverse effects as is evident by the mental state of most of the teachers who fell upon such laughter.

"NOOO, really! I wish I was there to see it." The lazy voice of the lotust one said, after he wiped clean his mouth from the laughter and began to munch an apple. A bunch of apples in plastic bag were on the bench next to the lotust one. And Prohvark was hopeful now, he saw his mistake of not having bought ration on a picnic was relieved by his friend. As he stretched a starving hand towards the bag, the straightest one teased, took quickly the bag away and ran behind the bench to signify a friendly cover. While all of them giggled and the standest one kicked Prohvark on his rack as he was circling the bench for those delicious apples. It was like a game of musical chairs. With the laughter serving as music. And while the music still played, the best friend cheated and took the empty bench before a possible elimination.

"Alright, fatsoh. I will give it to youh. Alright. But listen a while. You have to whait, man," said the straightest, while also parading and panting around the bench obstinately. Prohvark was too tired and didn't make any attempt to snatch away the bag, so he just listened to his teasing old friend, knowing well he would give him an apple to eat. So Prohvark rested next to standest on the railing while the artificial sea seeped in and over those mineral rocks. Straightest shooed the best friend away from his seat, and he obliged, for there was a speech to come. There is often a friend in the group, the most childish and frivolous of them all. But at times, he has something serious to say or do, at least a matter of importance for him and he drops away all that childishness for that one instance. Like how it's in the thief's nature to partake in robberies very often and enjoy them, but when he is trapped in one of those heists and seeing no way out, he just drops the load of cash and makes a run for his life. The straightest dropped that load of apple on his lap as he was panting and took that seat and began his speech. Perhaps an explanation of some sort, on why the thief partakes in such acts. During half of the speech, he was panting and then it eventually died down.

"Is happle or peach more nutritious? Which is more beneficial for the human body? I never cared enough to obtain that information, No. I always go with something that's more apphealing to my tastes, you know, that which I enjoy more. What about you, Pro? That's always been the conflict, I suppose. Between intelligence and emotions, between rheasoning and emoting. And to crave or to abstain. If you know what I mean, No? We sometimes choose what only seems good to us. And sometimes we choose while in full knowledge. At least I can claim ignorance as of now, hmm. I may go as far as to stop myself from obtaining the information in regard to which is more nutritious so I can make it easier for myself to enjoy and have oranges every time. Does it matter whether it is more or less nutritious? Well, I could take the risk and might find out that orange in fact is more nutritious. But that won't make it more delicious for me than it already is. Makes me wonder...between dreams and reality. An answer which lays somewhat in between religion and science. What do you say, Pro?"

"Just give him the goddamn apple, man. The guy is hungry, what does he care," said standest.

Prohvark nodded his head, which created a crystal-clear mental picture of Ross in his mind. Perhaps the poor guy was tired all the time, he thought to himself. He also extended his hand towards the plastic bag in order to garner pity towards himself.

"No, Pro. You gotta answer. You will get the apple, anyways. But do you like them peaches better?"

Prohvark said he would rather first make enough money

before forming an opinion at all. And then he would be able to buy both apple and peaches and make a salad out of it for him to enjoy. A silly joke, which made all of them chuckle. As straightest was handing the plastic bag to Prohvark, lotust quickly snatched it away and threw it towards the artificial sea. There is also a friend in the group who is quite restrained at most times, yielding to most matters. But upon viewing an opportunity, in which he could create a temporary chaos, but a chaos he knows will be relieved and laughed at with a subsequent step, quickly snatches away on such an opportunity. Like a rich businessman who having enough cash at hand won't mind scrapping whatever his current plan was to pursue another which just happened to pop in his mind. He might say to himself, "Oh well, I thought of buying a car. But let's scrap that. Let's even sell the current one and buy a jet instead." So too lotust thought, as he threw that bag to a wide-open mouth of our protagonist, who in a slow motion of a hungry moving head followed after it into the artificial sea. A small splash of water from the plastic bag of apples first and then the huge body of our protagonist followed later. If one might have seen his open mouth towards the direction of the artificial sea, one would have thought he stood in awe of the beautiful sight of the sea. But the friends knew he was just hungry.

What had happened in the past, in the real world, was that the friend after throwing the bag had said they would go to have a steak instead. And since it was the last day of high school, lotust also felt chivalrous enough to say that he would pay for it as well. But who knows lotust might have been one of those friends who also for a full stomach and full opportunity can lie. And it was so, after they got done with the meal, with his chipped tooth he laughingly claimed he had forgotten the money at home. They all said they would pay him back for the prank, as they somehow squeezed by without paying. And the cashier at the counter probably cursed them whenever they were bought to mind all his life.

But now in the underground, Prohvark deliberately jumped into the sea for he sensed his way out of this event. And it was not like at the grassy plain that he wished to escape out of dread, but he escaped with a longing of being back on top and paying a quick visit to his beloved friends. He also feared that they might disappear. An unexpected calamity of some sort. He did not want to waste any second to give an occurring chance to such a calamity anymore. Of a tight hug he wished, in between the crevice of which was not even space for ants lest a disaster. So he dived below, knowing well the bedrock won't be as deep and the chances of him laying his hand on that plastic bag of apples were good as well. As conveniently short as the distance between his hand and tummy. The bag of apples glowing heavenly red in the dark layers of the sea was as if kept heavy on a mine, upon releasing it the elevator exploded to sight from beneath the bedrock. And it led him down again, but he was happy that he had a stomach full of apples for whatever came next in store for him.

6

The elevator which bought our protagonist below was of a very special kind, the interior only to be realized if a mixture of the deep-sea water near the bedrock was mixed in with the water at the surface. And the formula to be frozen concrete. And then to cover with transparent sliding door, which reflected in itself a view of the fragment of that frozen sea and also Prohvark munching on those apples, oblivious to the beauty of the elevator space taking him down. He was in the elevator, like one at the theatre munching on soft drinks and popcorn, all the while the movie was getting over and then to go around asking questions in regard to the nature of what was playing on screen. So too as the elevator stopped, and the door slid open, Prohvark looked around in confusion.

He walked on out, and the elevator behind him disappeared into the ground again. He was faced with a straight pathway filled with moist ground, which looked like it was just being prepared for grass to be grown. A pathway leading straight ahead, surrounded by walls on either side of the shoulder. In between there was about space for three people to walk and no more. It was a maze. A maze much more generous than a footpath which only allows for two people to walk, making feel the one trailing behind un-listened to. Prohvark slid out his foot delicately from the shoe and pushed it against the ground. He felt that cold slightly wet sand around his sole, it crept up and onto his foot by about a millimeter. He forced his leg down, it went to about an inch and no further. Finding himself all alone with the tightness of the wall around him, perhaps he felt once again in his familiar apartments again, for he began to speak loudly to himself.

"OH, GREAT!" he said, as he kicked the sand, which sprinkled on the walls and collapsed back to the ground.

"Like this place was not a maze enough already. Now I am faced with a real one. You think I did not realize I was in one, HUH? HUUUUH? Now you are giving me clear signs. I am not such an idiot, ya know." He kicked the sand again to signify that in fact he was not. But the sand fell the same on the ground. Now he began berating the walls.

"What aboutchyu? What you giving me that blank stare for." He kicked the wall rather roughly, either thinking the wall was on the verge of collapsing or he greatly overestimated his leg muscles. So with a hurting leg, he still managed to keep talking, "That's right. I would have kicked you again, if not...uh...if not for mercy. Would have kicked you with the other leg, if you have a premonition that my left is hurting. Would have punched you. What you looking at? You dumb rock. The mountain has discarded you. The earth, the ground has discarded you. You have no friends. You hear me? You hear me there!"

He looked around to file a complaint and lend some words to other intangible objects. So looking up at the sky, who was perhaps cowering in fear, he felt the sky was alright, so he said, "You are cool. You are okay. You have all of us under your grasp." Feeling contented that since his complaint was deposited, perhaps there might come feedback of a solution, he began walking straight ahead. The pathway at the end was not clearly visible whether it was turning to the left or right. As he grew closer in distance, he saw it was turning to the left for him, but for the woman who was walking from the other side, it was a right.

"Ah, it's a left!" he said out loud.

"Ah, it's a right!" said the girly voice.

For a second, Prohvark appeared astonished and tapped with his forefinger the Adam's apple on his throat. And made a cough for assurance of a normal voice. The woman on the other end coughed and did the same which confused both of them again. Prohvark now pulled his shirt away from the body and spoke into the space between his tummy and the pulled-out shirt. The woman did the same. But the voice from Prohvark's mouth slid and wavered between the lines of his tummy, while the woman had a flat stomach, which made all the difference in the pitch. They understood that the turn held a different person. And they treaded quickly at such a possibility.

"Ah, so there is someone else here."

"Ah, so someone else is here."

They stood halted in front of each other in synchronicity as well. For a moment, Prohvark thought that she was mimicking him like how children usually do. But both of them laughed together at the same time at such a possibility. She laughed a little bit more than he did, which put all confusion to rest.

"Where are you headed?"

"Where are you headed?"

"Oh, come on now already. Alright, I am trapped here for quite a while now. Looks like there is not a way out. It's been an hour maybe. Or maybe more. My goddamn clock has stopped working for some reason. And you are the first person I see. Perhaps, you are the compass I need. So how long have you been here? Or wait...do you know the way?"

Prohvark said that he had just arrived at the maze. None of them bothered asking each other how they had reached here. Like they knew they both had fell from the sky. There are times when two people, two strangers, often find themselves in the same pinch of a salt bowl. In the same troublesome scenario, so their first and foremost priority becomes to find a way out. Regardless of who the person might be. An enemy or a friend, wise or dumb. They must help each other. And in such a case, wondering about the person's character or stories from past life becomes an exercise in fatality to time. Two enemies could find themselves in a prison of a third enemy. So they don't mind working together for a while. In this case, the third enemy happened to be the entrapping maze. But Prohvark only said he was very confused as well, and he omitted the retaliation against the maze when he went about torturing the sand and the wall.

"Hmm. I swear I heard a screaming voice a few moments before. But I am not too sure. You see, I have a very poor ear. It's my left one. Sometimes when people speak to me, I feel like they are whispering to themselves. So if you mind, as we walk, walk to my right, to the good ear." "Okay. Alright."

"Well, now. Let us go back the way you came. You see, because I have already walked from this path. You know. Perhaps, there will be luck on the other side," said the woman.

Prohvark agreed. He was way too confused to hold an opinion. And in a way it didn't matter which way he walked, for both of them were without instructions. It was a case of— whoever advises first gets the cake. So they walked back that turn of repetition. Prohvark had a slight hope that the elevator would be back in its place. But it quickly subsided when he realized so far the elevator never appeared twice at the same spot.

"You seem to be sweating a bit. Why? It isn't hot at all."

Prohvark was drying from the dive he took for the apple in the artificial sea which led him here. But since he didn't want to go in depth of that story, he just said that he was a victim of some kind of condition which made him sweat while nervous. The woman chuckled at that.

"Oh, are you nervous? And why is that, I wonder. Afraid, you might not find the way out. Or afraid that you find yourself alone with a woman in closed quarters."

"Oh, it's the latter. But they are sweats of fear because you must look at yourself in the mirror."

The woman laughed at that. They were talking to each other without offense, free and flowing, like they had known each other for a long age. Or perhaps, the enemies were teasing each other lest their friendship deepens to an extent whereupon they won't be able to hate or kill each other when the triple-threat is eliminated. After a while, they started discussing the nature of the maze. The walls and how the aging cracks stood out on some of those white, greying bricks. And how the walls seemed like a better canvas to paint upon in comparison to the sky. The sand, how it felt better than walking on the beach. One can walk on coals happily if there is another hand holding his. Especially if the guiding hand walks on normal ground. They talked about the small patches of grass growing against the wall. And once a bird flew overheard and the woman shouted after it comically for directions. Whereupon Prohvark replied for the bird in a birdy voice, "The hell should I know. The sky is like a directionless maze for me too." And they laughed silly, even though they felt a spark of relation, of company with that flying bird.

Now all of a sudden, she took a blue-inked pen out of her pocket and began playfully writing something on the back of Prohvark's shirt. He kept looking over the shoulder. And tried making out the words and letters by how the pen flowed and felt on his back. But he failed miserably. She got done and resumed walking besides him, smiling and looking down pretending she had done nothing. And Prohvark saw from her face that she meant to keep it a secret. So he bothered not asking, but hoped that somehow he will be able to make her say or she would do so herself. They walked for a while, and now the writing on his back was bothering him much more than the maze. So he kept looking for a mirror to read it. And there was not a mirror in that maze, for it was not a beauty parlour and they were very average-looking. A sudden urge to take off the shirt crossed his mind.

But he did not yet make an attempt. For a while, he lurked around trying to hide his tempting agony.

And the woman did not budge as well. They were also no longer talking about any matter at all. Maybe she did so on purpose to intensify the weight of that shirt on him. Maybe, she wanted him to take it off, so she could make fun at that tummy of his. Now, whatever was written on the back, Prohvark perceived it a poem of love, for his feelings were on the verge of that line. And the poem seemed to manifest itself into a heavy tangible object, a burden upon him, wearing him down physically. Only reading it could set his mind at ease. She definitely realized the misery of his position. And took delight in it. At the same time, pretending, putting on an act of "Unaware". Maybe she did not. But our hero, who possessed by the spirit of Romeo, was certainly projecting it to be so. He felt the curse and thought of certain individuals who regret getting a specific tattoo on their bodies. "Maybe this is how they feel, this is how…"

Now he kept eyeballing each and every corner. Looking for any help that could provide with a reflection, an angle of his back which was giving him a hell. It was not a crowded place. And there was a very slim chance of coming across any other person who might read it out for him. And if there was, Prohvark would be unable to ask of such a request from a stranger. For another to read what's on the back of his shirt would be like to open a letter of privacy. He also thought in his pride that it would be considered cheating. It would take away the fun of reading it for himself or the essence of making her to say it out loud. He looked at her face, and again she appeared with a defiant expression. Now he desperately began to hope for a stranger. But even then, he thought what if the stranger is not worthy in appearance. He thought if it was his best friend, he would allow him. There was also the fear: what if that person trapped in the maze was angry or in a hurry and refused to read it out for him. For after all, one too many enemies to each other in a cage will not be as friendly. But he for sure would still risk requesting the stranger. And he finally decided in his head, "I have had enough of this awfulness. I wish for a person to walk by in the next five minutes. And since I have no means to find out if five have passed or ten, I must make a guess that they have. So what if someone else reads it out for me. It is still intended for me."

So saying that and exactly then a stranger was walking towards them about fifteen yards away. He was balding, wearing a loose, light orange, full-sleeved shirt, unbuttoned at the top. And clean black pants. There was a pair of sunglasses, pulled all the way and resting on his shiny head. It looked like the glasses had created a bridge in an attempt to lead the hair surrounding on both sides of the head to make their way back to the spot of insecurity. Like how one provides support for grapevines to climb on. The glasses did help the bald head from standing out in the forefront. Prohvark thought to himself, "Sometimes a person on his deathbed has lost all the strength to read the last will of his, which he had thought of reading out loud to his surrounding family when he was healthy. It's decided then."

Now he began to justify his request of asking a stranger to

read the poem on his back. He told himself that it was also good that only three were present in the maze, for it was a request if made somewhere public, there will be a dozen of people present to read the private letter. As if his back was a revered piece of art. A spectacle. And he also convinced himself that although the guy approaching was nowhere close in appearance to his best friend's, he still did not have the appearance of a homeless person or a dictator. When there are dictators, there are no homeless people to be seen. They make a good job of hiding their failures. And since the balding one was approaching, it was evident he was neither. It was decided then. The man was worthy enough to read. That was his judgement.

Our hero was studying all the circumstance, thinking to himself and luckily not out loud. But he made the error of staring at the approaching person right in his face for a while quite inappropriate so as to make a person uneasy. And the stranger did take notice of him as was evident with his raised eyebrows and wrinkly forehead, which further took the attention from his shiny forehead. Prohvark also noticed that the stranger had noticed him, and it was like meeting the woman on the first instance all over again, but this time with a person he had not a preference of. So Prohvark in an attempt to ease the tension smiled a helpless smile, an expression which lost people have on their faces when usually they approach you lost and ask for directions. So did the baldy also think that perhaps they were asking for a way out of the maze. But that was the last thing on Prohvark's mind. The maze had disappeared. He only wanted to know which way the pen and writing went. There was also a hint of fear brewing in the baldy, the kind of fear which comes with walking down a street alone at night and a car stopping by next to you. The fact he was alone and they outnumbered him, even though if one was a woman, physically weak, but what if she knew Martial Arts. The baldy himself was bit of an anxious person.

Prohvark shrugged that smile off, thinking that perhaps he had smiled for too long and the matter was becoming even graver and cautious. He wished for an affirmation from Ross, now he truly felt when matters got as complicated as this, then only an answer of nodding the head up and down or back and forth was the best. At about five yards of distance from the baldy, she quickly peeped at our hero's face with an expression that she knew what he was about to do. A defeat. "Goddamn cursed poems." Prohvark repeated twice in his head. At about three yards, our hero raised his arm forward in an attempt to halt the person and start the initiative. But he quickly dropped the hand back as he was reminded of Ross and how he looked like a waiter in front of Mike's door at the party. Perhaps even worse, someone who earns his bread and butter living as a beggared. A vagrant. But he was dressed rather nicely for such an impression. The baldy took notice of that flicking arm. And all three of them were standing still.

"Yes, Sir. What is it? Are you looking for directions?"

"No. My good sir. Not at all. There is only a quick tiny request. Would you be so kind to read it out for me?" said Prohvark, turning his back.

"Well, Sir. Why did you not care to read before buying the shirt?" asked the baldy, "You should read it, you know. What if instead of 'Sir' written upon the shirt, there is something else like 'non-binary'. Heiehei," he added in a scornful manner, after having thought of the request as some sort of a prank.

"My good sir. It was a plain shirt. But on my way here from the bus, some naughty kid on the backseat carved it out. And before I could catch him, the bus stopped and he was out." Prohvark explained in a genuine plea for help. Every second of not knowing what was written on his back was bearing him heavily down.

"Come on," he added, as he looked once again disconsolately at the stranger's face.

The baldy began to read. His lips were quivering and his eyes squinted tight as if in presence of a heavenly bright light. Prohvark attempted to read the lips before they could announce verbally the writing. He also attempted to make a slight hint out of his expression. But it was a hard attempt since our hero was a bit disconcerted by his shiny head, now closer in proximity. He finally looked at our hero, who thought now that the baldy looked confused, astonished and overwhelmed. "This is not a poem. This is something else," whispered Prohvark to himself, finalizing on his expression. The baldy now at once spoke resolutely.

"My good sir, I cannot read. I am unable to. I am uneducated."

Our hero felt an immense sense of betrayal. He stood there still with his back against the stranger, a twisted neck, and pleading eyes for him to read. All that contemplation and thrill not yielding fruit made him refuse to give up without a reading and looked at the baldy with an eye that implied it was possible to read, he just had to try. But the baldy shook his head to channel his ignorant state along with a smile. All this time, the woman's existence was quite forgotten due to the torment, but now after the stranger had spoken, she suddenly shifted to the forefront with a shriek of laughter, embracing her stomach with tight arms around it. Both Prohvark and the baldy turned towards her, and the baldy chucked a bit upon hearing that sudden, contagious laughter, which made Prohvark pierce at him with an immense anger and treachery like people do with a vendetta of a thousand years. He thought the baldy was chuckling at his defeat.

"Imbecile. Piece of shit," said Prohvark out loud, and once in his head.

The baldy looked at him in the eye and saw it was almost teary.

"Well, Sir. Just because I'm uneducated doesn't mean you have to call me that way." And saying that, he quickly paced ahead and squeezed in between the woman and our hero. Prohvark watched him walk away on the road they had just walked through. With the baldy walking away, so went away the dilemma of risking a reading by an oncoming stranger. A burden alleviated from our hero.

"I feel like swapping shirts with that guy," said Prohvark, still watching the baldy walking away who now turned to a left and gave sight only to a wall. The remark made her laugh again but not quite as much she did earlier.

"Well, you know. I have just written down some gibberish. They have no meaning at all. Some symbols I have jotted as well here and there. The poor guy probably thought it was a special foreign language mixed in with an alchemical code. But it's just gibberish. You can have a look yourself."

Prohvark was dumbstruck. In his disbelief and a shocked state, he did not really care to be shirtless, half-naked. And he did so in a jitter. The shirt now taken off, he flipped in his hands and laid his eyes on it. He saw mere wastage of ink. He saw that the wastage laid bare revealed his feelings without ever saying anything or holding true meaning. And he knew that she knew. It was a love letter without a meaningful word. A key that can fit any lock and connect the veins of heart required. It was a winning marble rolling through the chessboard and knocking the king out in a game of children. It revealed his feelings to the tiniest details, which could not be missed if she had the eye for it. Prohvark attempted to cover up the incident with reason, and fortunately for him, it arrived at a time of much need.

"You idiot. We have wasted so much time. And ink. We could have used the pen and dragged it along this godforsaken greying wall. Marked our way out and the places through which we walked. By now we would have been out. And that poor baldy along with us too. Now he is lost in there and no amount of education can be of direction."

"Okay. Okayy. Fine. Wear your shirt back, will you! I mean I might have wasted time, but you are stopping that shirt from being of good service to you."

So they began walking, marking the wall with a straight line of blue ink. Prohvark mumbled that he hoped for enough ink to lead them out. It can happen that a few lines of ink will reveal a universe inside of a human being, but miles of ink can sometimes fall short in maneuvering through the designs of physical world. But they had not much to walk and to their surprise, there was a grown tree right in the middle of the path. A tree whose branches went over and above the walls of the maze. A tree about which they knew not how it grew, but it did from the few drops of the artificial seawater dripping on the soil as Prohvark first made his entry. It was the very spot when he first took those few steps as he came out of the elevator. Prohvark climbed at this opportunity, like climbing on a camel in a barren desert which was to come. He climbed like an agile monkey, and truly, it was a sight to see, for although he was chubby, he made the climb as if sliding in a soppy bathtub. Once on the highest point, he memorized the entire map of the maze and saw towards the west, an open green field from which was made a doorway into the maze.

"I wished I had not told you to wear the shirt, Tarzan. It is a sight, you know. You just have to begin howling in the required manner," screamed the lady's voice gaily from below.

Prohvark looked down at her in admittance, he was in fact enjoying the view. A slight wind which was blocked by the walls below now kissed his face at this higher altitude and his hair too was softly blowing. He had already memorized the design and stood there on top, observing the maze vertically. The top few laid out inches of the wall were whiter than the ones standing vertically below. From the top, the walls went left and right. In the shape of the alphabets. There was L, T and E. A blockage in the form of an F. And from every angle, one could say there was an I. Overall, a person could spend a thousand years inside the maze if not for hunger or starving. Or if a possibility of such a life existed, he would spend a thousand years to no avail but one look from an attached vertical point of view would lead him out to an escape in no instant. It was a mixture of the same alphabets. Only a different outlook was required from the "I". When and how it twisted. And even the designs of the world were at the mercy of a few letters.

So Prohvark climbed back down to the lady's voice below. A bit clumsily now and he jumped from the last branch straight to the ground, his feet sinking further than an inch. He walked confidently towards the lady. And almost heroically offered his hand for her to lay on but sufficed with a few words of following instead. As they were walking on out, they felt no attachment to the place, for they were attached to each other. Perhaps, even the maze felt happy that way. A relation which he thought he created and wished for it to stay.

Prohvark took the first step on the open field of exit. And the elevator sprang from below. He turned around for a look in her eye. There was not enough space for two individuals to fit inside the elevator.

"Well, I bid you farewell. You do remember the other side of exit. It's towards the east. I think I will help you memorize the way one last time. And remember, keep tight to the pen. Don't overmark the walls. I feel horrible about the baldy. Perhaps, he would have accompanied us if not for my harsh words. Anyway, just lead yourself towards the exit. Hopefully, you will cross ways with him. If not, then once you are outside on the east, try throwing the pen above and further away in the maze. Maybe it will land on his head. Maybe it will fall on top of those walls and out of reach. But if that's the case, then truly luck was against him for the third time. A probability unlikely if one keeps attempting to persuade his luck. But if he grabs a hold of that pen, he might mark the walls in his own way to help him see the path which he has walked and not yet walked upon. Eventually, one of the unwalked paths will lead him out. That's it then."

"Thank you."

That was all she said. All that was required. For there is no better a way to depart than to lend a helpful, caring hand and in return have gratitude for the help. Our hero rested himself in the elevator. And leaned back against the wall which was enveloped by a design—a vertical view of the maze, endless. Looking straight ahead, he saw the lady smiling at him and he did so in return. And she quickly waved her hand and entered the passage to the maze. He went down, saying out loud to himself, "Hopefully, this is the last one."

7

Our hero almost arriving at his station was greeted with sand seeping in through the cracks of the elevator below. He slid his shoe over them and bit his teeth due to the sound of friction the sand created against the designed floor of the maze. He tried bending down and hit his head against the glass door, reminding him of the claustrophobic space he was in. So he squatted tight, his knees stacked against the door and he barely made the tip of his fingers to feel the sand. He felt the smooth grains and closed his eyes, imagined them to be sugar, which he would sprinkle in a hot cup of coffee on a winter, admiring the raindrops racing against the window. Sipping that delicious coffee, as the cars below were stuck in traffic. And he would see a lucky person with the window down, having his hot cup of coffee as well. And they would look at each other and nod. He imagined the driver had the same beautiful outlook of the traffic while stuck as he had from atop in a dissociative state. He opened his eyes to the glass door, behind which was darkness, perhaps the elevator was moving at such a speed it was hard to discern what it was, which was reduced to a shuffling darkness. Was he really traveling below earth's crust? If so, which level was this? Lithosphere? The mantle? He was unsure. Or was he travelling upwards and into space? If so, was it still the troposphere? Because he wished for a slight graze against an aeroplane's wing, which will break the elevator in half and he would drop down and land on the terrace of the building in which he lived as a tenant and hopefully he had a parachute to open. He looked at the glass door and sighed, "Whatever it is, no one in his right mind is going to believe this story. And for sure, my passage would have been easier with a cup of coffee."

But he was mistaken as he began to shuffle back to his feet and found he was helpless because he was stuck tight in that position, knees against the door and back against the wall. A turtle in its shell. He tried again but in vain. So he just waited for the door to open. He would have waited calmly if not for the realization that the sand was slowly creeping up to bury him alive and his ankles were already buried under its crept. So he began to panic and struggle for a stand up. If he would just have been standing, perhaps there would be enough time for his head to stick out until the elevator opened. No amount of coffee or any other drink would allow a person the peace of mind in order to tolerate such a burial. So he struggled and the squeaking sound of his knee muscles against the glass door just laughed at his efforts. He could not get up and the sand was now up to his shin and squatting navel. "IF ONLY I HAD BEEN STANDING." He screamed in that claustrophobic space. Now he no longer was able to struggle, for the creeping sand took away such an effort of the muscles. He laid his forearms on the sand and began to dig with his fingers in a panic. The sand had no other space to deposit itself into and soon it would cover the cylindrical shape of the elevator. The sand crept and crept, now it reached till his upper arms, almost to the shoulder. He began to gasp hard and held his hands up as if someone had a gun pointed at his throat. But it was only the golden sand under which his neck was drowning now. He felt heavy. Had trouble breathing, the sand against his neck was disconcerting. Now it reached till his poor trembling chin, hiding it. A tear fell from his eye and made a bubble in the sand and the grain found its way in there, to make it a glittering gold bubble which soon flattened out to merely a wet spot. He tilted his head sideways for a few seconds' leeway from being fed by the sand. And the sand crept onto our hero's thick earlobes and covered it along with his nostrils. The other ear felt burning hot in the open air. He began to clinch, opening and closing his fists continuously in a plea for quick arrival of the destination. The merciless sand almost reached till his left eye, and he felt his poor eyelashes against its grainy surface. He blinked furiously, the lashes beating against the smooth silky surface of the sand. Finally, he laid the left eye shut. The right open still staring hopefully at the door, which felt now like the door of heaven. If someone was to look at the helpless forehead of our protagonist sticking out of the sand, he would think it was a dwarf on the verge of being brutally buried alive, which somehow makes it sadder. The grave of a dwarf is much a sadder scene, for one thinks it's the grave of an innocent child. Or if one happens to be gloomily depressed on that specific occasion upon coming across the dwarf's grave, he would think the child was lucky enough to die a young death and escape the atrocities, the sufferings of life, again undermining all the hardship the poor buried dwarf went through. "Am I a joke to you?" sighing the dwarf in heaven. Prohvark could not move his hands, they were stuck stiff. Finally, the door slid as smoothly as ever, the required space was created for the sand to flow out. He coughed a mouth full of sand and exhaled deeply the suffocating grains out of his nostrils. And inhaled that much needed graceful air of still being alive and out of a deadly disaster. Stretching his legs to freedom, the sand slipped between the thighs. When he almost took ten breaths of relief, he realized he was finally out of danger. He realized that the door had opened and his butt cushioned now in peace, laughing victoriously at the leftover sand in the elevator. He let his hands drop onto the sand, clinched them a handful to throw them out the open door. He threw a handful more and cried, "Never again. Never again!" Then he inserted a hungry forefinger into his nostril and cleaned out those annoying brown grains. Doing the same with his left ear. And the right as well even though it did not taste the feel of that burying sand. At once, he stood up thinking to himself that was probably the last time he would ever squat. And the first preparation he would make if he ever made it back on the ground level was to replace the traditional toilet with a western one.

So thinking and with a normal rhythm of breathing, he stepped on out to the level which laid in front. But he could not really see much, for there was a heavy sandstorm brewing. He shielded his eyes with his palm and once again tried to see from between his fingers if anything could be seen to decipher. But it was only the wind howling. And his feet knew with the struggle it moved that it was submerged in sand. "A DESERT," he thought. The blowing sand stung against his face and ears. He began unbuttoning the flipping shirt which revealed half his abdomen to the torture as well, and his hands struggled against the sweeping wave of wind. The wind would not allow him to unbutton completely. It wrestled him down, and he was once again given a taste of that sand. Standing back up to his feet, it felt like the wind had amassed greater power as he struggled to maintain a straight direction. He swung like a pendulum. The force of the wind was such that it would have demolished to ground any wall, but it only made our hero appear for a moment like a part of it, swirling him in all directions. He felt he needed to cover his face, for that is where the delicate, important features lay. And if he had to make it through, he certainly needed the help of those. So he once again began to unbutton his shirt, this time successfully and wrapped it around his face. He figured the wind did not allow him to see anyway, so it was better to be in the dark but with the shirt wrapped around his head, serving as protection against the storm, a fragile armor for the priceless features of his face. He walked and walked. The wind howled, it was the master of opera, the conductor playing for an abandoned theatre and led the orchestra and whatever fell within its waving grasps to a blind destination. Prohvark was sure the piece had to end. He just had to stay strong until then. He was also sure of him being in a desert, so he walked without any fear of falling from a high precipice. But he was mistaken, as he happened to be on a high dune and the wind like a merciless enemy lifted him up for a rolling ride down the sand dune. Somewhere Mozart in his grave laughed his weird laugh, relating with the madness of the composition the opera was unfolding towards. But our hero had the last laugh, as the sandstorm began to take a rest and the sunlight managed to seep in. He had tightly clinched with his teeth the shirt against his face so that it did not unwrap and leave it bare while he rolled in a dramatic fashion.

Now laying defeated, he realized the foolishness of his attempt to make it through the sandstorm to a destination unknown. It was a tiring effort, a drill in vain. And it was mainly the fall from the dune which led him to the realization. So he laid there in one spot, nauseated. Quietly hoping that it would end. A headache was knocking on his forehead. And a sleep which was to awake him to a calm and contented desert.

It was a bit after midnight when our protagonist awoke. In front of his vision, the triangle roof of a tent. A part of it in the corner was grey and hanging torn. He felt the sand crumbs in the corner of his lips; some fell between his teeth for him to grind upon. He turned to the right and saw the back of a figure looking at the bonfire lit below. The light from the fire revealed his great white beard from the sides. And a streak of red clearly stood out. There was a blanket in which Prohvark was tucked tight. He removed it from his body and felt the cold breeze of the night desert, which compelled him to sit beside the fire as a companion with the man whose face he had not yet seen. He crawled towards the fire and the yellow orange bright spots. Once besides the old man, our hero was much more captivated by the burning flames, which occupied his first glance. It was only after the old man offered him a water bottle wrapped in a maroon cloth that our hero looked at the bottle first and then to the friendly face of the stranger who nodded with a smile. Prohvark loosened the cap, once again focused on the fire and drank those refreshing sips of water. The fire seemed so beautiful that even if it would have burned the sheltering tent, they would not have wasted any water upon it. Even in possession of a fire truck. There is a certain primitive beauty in fire that none can replace. A beauty equaling to the sunsets and the sunrises, the waves of sea crashing on the shore, being in the presence of your naked first love. One can watch the best movie in the world for a time of three hours, maybe four, while surrounded with friends, but he might fall asleep during it or might request to watch the rest later. But in the presence of such a beautiful fire such as the one burning in tent, even two strangers will forget their strangeness towards one another. And they might sleep next to the raging fire without putting it off, the same they would not have done with the movie screen. So the two strangers sat there and listened to the story the fire was narrating for a while.

The old man seemed to be above sixty years of age. He had a messy long beard which reached to his collarbone. The fire was gleaming in his eyes. And the whites of it stood out. He was of tanned skin and looked like a man who had travelled a lot. The tanned skin could have been a consequence of the desert or spending time far too long pondering about the beauty of fires while seating next to their frying heat and being consumed by them. His white moustaches twisted on to the sides of his beard, away from falling onto his lips. It was a superior, classy moustache unlike that of the teacher. His lips were slightly darker than the color of his skin, helping them to have an existence of their own. His eyes spoke of themselves as being in a careless, always smiling, reverie. But eyes that could shift at ease, smoothly, at any sign of disturbance. Supposing the fire had just died out, his eyes would reveal in themselves a scream questioning why. And once the reason was revealed, they would in a jitter go back to their original reverie. His eyebrows drooped lazily at the ends, still consisting partly of black hair. Black hair which reminded any watching eye of the beautiful face he had once in his youth for sure. There was not a visible scar on his face; nevertheless, his face painted a picture of a man who had been through a lot of struggling wars in his lifetime. Overall, he looked like a man who had a lot to say, many a stories, but missing a companion's ear by the fireside, he held on to them. He looked like a man whose words were much needed, and it was true. For as he opened his mouth for the first words, our hero forwarded an inch not only his ears but his whole body at the direction of the sitting old man. Prohvark was sitting to his right, rather than to his straight, which gave him a clear view of the old man's face without the flames of the smokeless fire getting in the way. As he began to speak, the fire crackled a bit higher as if the fire too was waiting, unknowingly for the old man to speak.

"I have been here for a long, long time. Oh, this desert. Me and this fire. When I slept, he was extinguished as well. When my eyes were open, it was as if he was burning for me. I sleep in the night, he sleeps in the day. I walk and sweat during the day, and the sun, the revenging sun acting like his forefather, punishing me for working him so hard. I pleaded once to the sun to understand. I told him, ;Heyyy, maan. The fhayar is willing. There is no fhorce I use. We are two willing companions on a short road.' But the sun never listens. Having no ears, like the fire over here. Anyway, my friend, from where have you fallen? So much for the fire. I have introduced you to my friend. Now it might be your turn. You know, it's good. It's good that I will listen to a human's voice. After so long listening to the fumes of this fire and it's crackling. So begin. If you don't want to speak of yourself, speak of the weather. Huehuehue."

When the old man laughed, his whole body heaved up and down. It was a hearty laugh. Although not contagious, it would definitely put a smile on the opposite face. Prohvark was at a loss on how to begin. He said a few things about his life. Although it was an empty life able to be surmised in a few sentences, he tried elongating to hide his shame. And purposely stuttered and paused between sentences to make it seem that he had spoken for a good time. As for how he ended up in the desert, he just said that he had lost the way. He said he was thirsty, looking for some water and he remembered people always talking about the beautiful oasis which are found in the hearts of desert. Although it is not found precisely and geographically at the centre of a desert, it is still the heart of desert. Like a human being is considered alive if the heart is beating. So the word 'Desert' cannot be said without a mental image of the oasis coming to imagination.

"Ah, the oasis. The oasis. Which increases tenfold the beauty of the bonfire besides it. There is one not so far away from here. Where I fill up my drinking waters from. Heavenly water. A caravan passes through once in a while. Mostly tired. Unable to talk and tell stories. So I let them be. And when they awake in the morning, they always seem to be in a hurry of leaving. As if the oasis had sharks in it. Huehue. Or as if the desert was running short. Anyway, now you are here. Awake. And it's not morning yet, so you must be in a hurry to leave. So we can be content in our speaking. We have caught the shark by its tail.

Huehue."

Prohvark focused on the fire. And the old man began singing, humming an old tune, a tune with a depth as if it was portraying the whole of human stories and existence up until current moment. The humming acted like background music to the movie, the fire in front. The old man reached for a cloth besides him and unfolded it, revealing to sight a two-and-a-half kg fish. A fish enough to fill two stomachs. An old man generous enough to not bat an eye. And a fire thirsting for its juices. And the sun was not in the way. The cold breeze was like heaven.

"You know," began the old man, as he thrust in a sharp stick in the mouth of the dead fish, whichexited around the corner of its tail. And the stick's end, he dug partly into the sand in front of the fire. He surrounded the sticks with stones of support to stop it from falling over. And the raging fire was already turning brown the fish for eating.

"You know. The oasis nearby is tiny. A man passing through, a thought pass in him to sit for fishing. But I know. Every time I am there, there is always a fish to catch. Never have I returned empty handed. Once I caught a large, laaaarge red fish. Not the size of a shark, for I would have run. But...uh...yeah, here. Just like the fish here. A bit tinier. A shiny red fish with a yellow tail. And dark red fins. What a beauty. In awe, I almost dropped it back to freedom. Huehue. Then I quickly jumped on to sand and stood for a while admiring its beauty as it was struggling, flipping in my hand. And it was beautiful even when dead silent. Ah, the shiny scales. I could have sold it for a good price to one of those caravans and catch myself a regular one. But I just felt it too special. Maybe against the back of my hand, it seemed even better. A hand which was to devour rather than trade it away. It was good. It was good that I held on to it. I enjoyed frying it better than I did the rest. The red skin was magnificent under this fiery light. Never have I caught a fish like that again. But I will remember the one forever. A shabby-looking person from a caravan requested me to trade. I will also remember his denied expression. Huehue. He said, 'I will pai yu goood, old mhaan.' I just told him that I already had a lot of treasure hidden away under the sands which no one would ever find after my death. Huehuehue. You can pocket your coins. And I walked away."

The frying fish turned brown on the side. The old man flipped the wooden stick and put the stones back into a holding place. The side away from the fire now was already cooked and the smell from the meat occupied the tent.

"Now for this side. You don't speak much, do you? Or am I not giving you the chance? Forgive an old man. And make listen a young. Always. So anyway, I bought that red fish back to the tent here. And cooked it as we are doing now. But you were absent that time. Huehue. Regret not. The meat was not as delicious as it looked. There was no justice in there. It was like a bitter woman you saved from the sea. The one cooking here looks to have a better taste. But it was truly a sight. What a sight. The red skin of the fish as it turned brown. Just like the one here. But very different. It was like watching a young beauty of twenty-one turn to seventy in a matter of twenty minutes. I marveled at it. Magnificent! I pulled it away from the fire when one side was completely brown. And looked in awe, wishing for the red skin to spread all over again. So I could watch the chain of decaying beauty in a plain sight again. But it was not possible. Sadly. The brown and red skin seemed like sun and moon now. And I directed the sun towards the path of moon again. As I flipped that beautiful side for this fire to devour. In a matter of minutes, the fish was unrecognizable and my appetite had completely taken over. In a matter of minutes, only my full stomach existed. Huehue."

The old man lifted the stick from the sand. And the stones he laid in a half circle besides the fire. He placed a white cloth in between himself and Prohvark and laid the cooked fish upon it. Then he took out a sharp knife and precisely made two halves of the fish for them to suffice their hunger with.

The fire's light falling over the fish and the fish resting upon the white cloth made it appear like a 3D painting. And every bite they took was like taking the brush back to first stroke. The old man carefully munched on the fish. A bone on his first bite, he sucked on the meat and forced his head backwards, pulled out the bone and threw it in the fire. Prohvark had not eaten fish for a long time. He ate in a hurry, unmindful of the bones sticking out. Food can be eaten either by hand or spoon but a fish always without bone. The old seeing the hurry of our hero began to converse in the middle of a chewing bite. And as his tongue struggled with the meat, the first sentence which was important came out as gibberish.

"Begh kharful wiht da bhoens. They can create a problem. Huge problem. Huger if a huge bone. The fish is mighty delicious. Our burning friend here has done a magnificent job. I would have patted it on the back like I did my son. But my hands are without proper covering. Huehue. I had a son once, you know." Here he quickly swallowed the meat in his mouth without proper chewing. "But he went another way. He could have been the one in front of me, enjoying the fish. He was as hot-blooded as this fire. He had this quarrel with a child of his age. Oh, children! And their blood boiling. Magnificent. Never a combination which does them good immediately. Only after years when they grow old. But you have to be alive for such a fruit to eat from. So the quarrel, the arguments went for a quite a while. And it ended bad. Very bad, you hear me. It ended with bad blood. My son, that stupid idiot, he killed the other child on a cold night. You hear me. As the bonfire was raging, here, like just here. The other child was sleeping. My son, that idiot, which I struggled to raise, he entered the tent. Made a loud noise. On purpose. On purpose. So the other poor child could wake up and see who it was that came for him. Blood boiling, a *baaad* combination. So my child, my child! He did that sinful deed."

Here, he paused momentarily to have a look at the fire. And the fire brimmed in his poor old sad eyes. But looking back at the fish shining on the white cloth, the trace of sadness quickly went away. Now his eyes only prepared for the next bite he was going to take. And to resume the story, he was telling. His tongue struggled again.

"So mkhy chidld, kilslls the poooh child. (He swallowed the rest of the bite without proper chewing). Now my child lived a few good years in hiding. And then died a natural death. I buried him myself along with the one who bought me the news, his friend next to me. And I have lived for far too long. Not only have I gone through my beloved son's death but also through the death of the one, his friend, who bought me the news. Magnificent! Anyway, I buried him like the murderer he was. But I prayed for his forgiveness. I did. Now what happens? Bad blood. The father of the murdered child came revenging after me. After all those years. He saw now that my son had died. But his need for a revenge did not. It only shifted directions from boiling blood to whatever mine is. Boiling spoiled milk, I suppose. Huehue. Probably it was not the old man of the murdered who wanted revenge himself. But was persuaded by people around him. Anyway, he came looking after. Came with a short sharp knife. I turned around in time, and the stab pierced my upper arm. I grappled him by the shoulder. And we went rolling down the dunes. The sand buried the bloody knife. My blood fell in his eyes. And I followed with a punch to his mouth, which broke his teeth. A caravan passing just in time saved us from each other. Good caravan. Beautiful camels. Magnificent!"

Here he stopped to take a few gulps of water down his dry throat, which was about tired from so much speaking. And the fish on his side of the cloth was heavily remaining, for he had been busy with a talking mouth rather than a chewing one. Nevertheless, our hero enjoyed better his mouthful of fish with the story. Prohvark requested the bottle for himself, and as he drank, the old man looked at the side of his cloth and saw only bare bones, the painting was almost stripped too. So he kept a part of his fish on the other side for Prohvark to eat. Perhaps, the old man thought a mouthful would much better invest in the narration of his story and will stop our hero from interrupting him. He began again.

"So, the good caravan broke us apart. Magnificent! And everything was clear as day. There were trials and it took a short time. But he was in jail for attempted murder. Later, I went to visit him behind the bars. We conversed, crying. He admitted his grave mistake. I visited him quite a few times. It's strange how two rivals out to kill each other are a sentence away from saving each other's life forever. We made good friends. I went around pleading with the courts to forgive his actions. I forgave him myself. But the court did not. I maintained my pleadings of pardon for a couple of years to no avail. They said they worked by fixed rules and not individual relationships. At last, I got tired. And I went to my friend, I told him of the ordeal. I told him even I had wasted quite a significant amount of time running around. And perhaps years of thinking about it. He understood. He was happy he made such a friend while behind bars. The poor father wished if he could turn back time, he would replace me and get rid of the people around who persuaded him to act on revenge. Magnificent. Right, all this debacle in the end made me hate the stupidity of my murdering child even more. Throughout the ordeal, and specially, after the time my friend attacked me with the knife, I was asking myself,' Why should I, a father, pay for his sins?' It was not me who took away the life. I was left confused at the mystery to fathom. For I did ask forgiveness for his sins. And then it was hard, more hateful an act for me to forgive my son after I made friends with the man who almost murdered me. For the dead child's father would often speak about how sweet his son was and occasionally how he would act righteously. Anyway, if I could ask forgiveness for the sins of my child, then in a way was I also liable to pay for it? Was it the same thing? I stopped cracking my head over it one of those days, staring at this fire, yeah right here. I said if God can forgive a dead man's sin by the prayers of one alive, then he also is powerful to make a living one pay for the crimes of the dead. And since God is all justice, all knowing, then it must be that the people below were in some way connected to the happenings. Maybe I am responsible for my child killing the other poor child, as much as my own son is. Anyway, here I am now enjoying fish with a stranger. I find it funny how people can often boast left and right of sacrificing their lives for the loved ones, and when the time comes—poof. Nowhere around. Huehue. God does work in mysterious ways."

Our hero had already eaten the fish to bare bones. He sat legs extended and reclining with the help of his hands. And the old man's side of the cloth still had fish left enough. He nodded as an offer, our protagonist shook his head in refusal. The old man now finding himself alone on the cloth began to eat in a hurry, an act which he early advised our hero against, in a gargle while chewing it himself. Now he began to speak again.

"It's magnificent! The world is as mysterious as this fire, here, yeah right here, burning in the middle of the desert. And…We are like…sands…odkdms….cukhh…khuaqak…!!!"

On that cold breezy desert night, the old man who warned others to be weary of fish bones himself carelessly ate the fish too quickly. As well as tried his luck a few too many times with an open mouth while talking loudly. A massive fish bone stuck in his throat, he choked till death, breathing his last. Such is life, one minute eating a delicious fish, the next, tongue dead, unable to proclaim there are many a plenty fish out there at sea. For the one which truly mattered to you, yourself, is the one number, the one fish counting less. And our hero looked upon the sight in a reverie, like the old man's i   death too was a part of the story he   had been narrating. The full stomach was weighing him down. But he quickly jumped to his senses, and before he made an attempt of helping the poor old man with the bone in his throat, he saw in his wide-open eyes the fire was no longer brimming. And his hands clasped his throat, in a sad state of affairs, implying that he had partly been responsible, sinful for his own death. Our hero bent down beside him and once again drank from the bottle which the old man had first offered him. Then he let go of his hand lazily over the old man's face, shutting those expressionless eyes for the grave sand to not seep in. Perhaps the sand hid many of the old man's treasures, but he himself was something that the sand would never hide. Coins are only beneficial in hand, and the sand slips from between the fingers. Coin under the sand is non-existent, a dead body under it forever lives in memory. The old man's beard still slightly moved with the breeze of a world moving on, the wind wanted to flow for as long as it could around this companion which lay dead now. The bonfire was almost dead on its way towards glowing coals and the morning sun was beginning to light that golden desert. But the old man's body under the sand would no longer be a subject to the rays of the defeating sun with which he once bargained. It was truly magnificent!

Prohvark picked up that lifeless body. Laid it on his shoulders and went out of that homely tent in which they had spent almost the entire night talking. He walked a distance away from the tent, and when the body began to weight him down feeling heavy, he dropped it on the sand. The crooked pocketknife of the old man with which he cut the fish into two equal pieces, he kept it on his unmoving chest. Our hero began to dig the grave in the middle of the desert, as the first rays of the morning sun were helpfully shedding light on how many more inches to dig. It was not a tough task to accomplish. The soft sand gave in freely to his attempt at burying the old chatty friend. And in no time, the pit was more than enough for the old man and his beard. Prohvark laid the body on his shoulder again and jumped into the hole, laying it down softly. He picked up the knife, it still had the smell of cooked fish emitting from its blade. Our hero had a last look at it and wondered at all the things the old man must have torn through during his time. Prohvark thought of pocketing it and keeping it as souvenir, for the memory. The knife also seemed strange and slightly antiquated. But he let the thought subside, and wiping the knife with his shirt, he placed it on the chest again. Then he folded the old man's hand onto the chest; the palms were resting on the blade. The old man looked like a mighty warrior, a legend who had just died a natural admirable death and who went around slaying heavily armored soldiers armed with spears by himself using just that tiny blade. Prohvark thought it was a good memoir to bury in the grave with him, for it was a blade, the final act of which was spent in dividing a brotherly meal between two strangers. The blade was an appetite-fulfilling thorn.

Prohvark, down on his knees, began to shove sand into the pit. He thought it was a great thing the old man died, for the horrible possibility of being buried alive also died along with him. He shoved the sand and restrained himself a look at the old man's face. He stubbornly looked at the feet, unable to swallow such an end for an amicable face. After carrying on for a couple of minutes, he had a look at his efforts. He saw the entire torso had already vanished beneath the heaps of golden sand. He worked quicker at filling the rest of the pit, for he felt the most appealing part about the old man was already gone and tarnished. In no time, the desert seemed whole. The old man had become a part of it. Although not specifically by name, he also had a share along with every mention of the desert in books of Geology. Our hero would certainly be reminded of that magical beard upon hearing or looking at images of desert. But upon viewing the sand, he would only get pangs of nervous anxiety, perhaps the fear of being buried alive will make him wish for a death sooner.

Prohvark would also be reminded the basic etiquettes of consuming fish, as the elevator sprang back up again from the same spot which was the grave of the old man. The walls of the elevator depicted a painting of the skeleton of ten red fishes, the eatable part missing, only the tail and the head with its mouth open revealing sharp teeth. It was the red fish which the old man had spoken very highly of. In the depiction on the elevator wall, it was missing the required grandiose of a looking eye, upon which our hero mistakenly thought that old people often used to exaggerate the beauty of things. Our hero tapped the elevator door with his foot and the door slid open. It was the glass door which took away the shine from the scales of the depicted fish. Now Prohvark saw that indeed it was a magnificent fish. A fish worthy to have a back against. He stepped below into the pit, the only time he had to lay down horizontally while travelling in the elevator. He felt a very strange connection now with the old man. He thought to himself, perhaps even the old man was laid on his way somewhere to a destination unknown. As he thought this, the elevator door slid tight. He was on his way towards being delivered to the very familiar grounds when we began first in the story. He was to be delivered back to the top. The last level he had just been through.

PROLOGUE

Prohvark awoke on his bed in his familiar quarters. The paint of the roof had taken a beating throughout years of humidity and changing seasons. A part of it flaked off and fell right on his lips, which stopped him from continuing the lazy stupor of wasting any further time in bed. He sat on his squeaky bed and thought he might paint over the walls. Maybe with a bright, lively colour. He thought of pink. The fact that he was back on surface and in familiar settings did not surprise him, nor did he wonder about the mystery of the world he had just went through. He just knew what had to be done.

Going up to the window to have a look at that nameless building, the chair was in the way. He kicked it energetically towards the corner to show dominance. The window brought to sight a sunny late morning. A couple of birds flew in grace, flying like the sun shone for them and all eyes were beholding them. Prohvark had a good look at the nameless building across the diametrical roads. He held steadfast in his intentions. And in five minutes, he was down and out on the edge of the road, waiting for a clearing to make his way towards the office. Approaching the entrance to the building, he spotted the cleaner brushing the floor who looked at him and smiled a friendly smile. Prohvark nodded his head.

He took the elevator towards the office, and in a moment the cubicle was in sight. Ross and Rodric saw him approaching, besides them the empty seat on which the Mike of an inferior position used to sit. They hurried him on.

"Where were you? Took you long. You know the assistant was just bluffing, right. He has not the necessary power to fire or hire. But let's hope he does not overhear me demeaning his capabilities. Who knows what might happen then. Take the seat. Get to work."

Ross nodded and went typing. Prohvark shuffled over the staplers and the papers on his worktable, he was trying to get hold of all that was required to move out of this place once and forever. A pack of yellow chewing gum he pocketed in the front of his shirt. There was an old, rusted coin which he kept for good luck. He deposited the coin into the back pocket of his pants. A couple of cards with numbers which were of help in possible scenarios. He kept shuffling the contents upon the table and beneath it to look for anything which he might regret having have left over. And that which will force him to possibly come fetching for it once again towards this dreadful place. He wanted to nullify the chances of such a revisit from happening again.

"You know. You could sit on the desk and shuffle those things around. You pretending to work will appear much more believable then. By the way, I overheard talks of a possible hiring of a newcomer.

It's a lady. She might soon be joining us here on this desk, which once belonged to our beloved Mike. Hopefully, she is a smoker. And her taste is good. I don't want to smoke on low-quality cigarettes."

"I'm quitting, Rodric. I'm done."

Rodric and Ross both looked at him with pursed lips. They told him it was a bad decision. For a promotion could be around the corner any second now. To put weight to their claim, both of them pointed at the same time towards the aluminum door which now housed their old colleague, Mike. Prohvark just shook his head and got a hold of all that was required for him to finally leave. He had one last look of indifference towards those age-old colleagues. And there was a look in his expression which conveyed to them that perhaps they had to do the same. That they were wasting a precious time in hopes of something which was not worth it. Prohvark had taken two steps towards the exit when Ross called out to him. It was a long time since our hero could remember any vowels coming out of his mouth.

"Prohvark, what will you do now?"

"I don't know, Ross. I don't know. I might come over once again tomorrow to have a look at the woman who is gonna replace Mike as our colleague. I too heard about her. I have a feeling she is someone I know. But I quit. I might later go on a vacation. To a quiet, green place. Try getting in touch with a couple of old friends. See what they are up to. Hopefully, they are breathing. What I know for sure is that I don't want to grow old in this place, in this lifeless building. As a friendly advice, and I know I have not given much or any of this to both of you ever. But If I were you, I would consider thinking about doing the same. Quitting. Goodbye. Good luck."

Prohvark was almost at the door of his exit when the assistant's voice boomed after him.

"Where do you think you are going? Squeezing out on a couple of working minutes?"

"I quit," replied Prohvark with a wave of the hand, without turning around and stopping his feet from movement.

The assistant thought of it as a joke first. No way he thought someone could find the soul to quit after so many soul-crushing years in this place. But when he saw our hero was almost at the threshold of disappearing from sight, he screamed after him.

"You don't quit. You are fired. Yeah. Get out of here. I told you I was gonna pay you back for that rocketing stapler which you aimed with a pinpoint painful accuracy towards the middle of my head. It's your head now. You are fired, you hear me? I will shout until you have entered the elevator. I know you are waiting there for it to come up. Yeah. There is the ding of the door opening. You are fired. Yeah. There is the ding of the elevator going down. Good riddance."

He muttered to himself weakly that his job was now made difficult, for he had to find another replacement for the empty seat left behind by our hero. What a busy week it was, he told himself. One got promoted, then he had to make amends filling that vacant spot left by the promoted and now another just got fired by his hands. In a lazy thought, he said to himself that perhaps it would be good if he demoted Mike and brought him back to his older position, except now he would occupy Prohvark's seat. He mused over this idea, and slowly, it was starting to appear favourable, as he did not want to risk the burden of managing two newcomers at the same time.

As for Prohvark, it remains to be seen whether he walked the walk or whether he floated the float or swum the swim. Perhaps, the reader might take it upon himself, imagining the end of our hero's adventures. Perhaps, he might undertake such a journey himself. As for Ross, nothing can be said about him, unless and until he nods.

Printed and Bound by *Passive Printers* - www.passiveprinters.com
Printing press that offers Print on Demand (POD) Facility.
Printed in The Islamic Republic of Pakistan.